QADDAFI'S
POINT
GUARD

QADDAFI'S POINT GUARD

THE INCREDIBLE STORY OF A PROFESSIONAL
BASKETBALL PLAYER TRAPPED IN LIBYA'S CIVIL WAR

ALEX OWUMI
with DANIEL PAISNER

RODALE.

Rodale books may be purchased for business or promotional use or for special sales.
For information, please write to:
Special Markets Department, Rodale Inc., 733 Third Avenue, New York, NY 10017.

Printed in the United States of America

Rodale Inc. makes every effort to use acid-free ♾, recycled paper ♻.

Book design by Christopher Rhoads

Library of Congress Cataloging-in-Publication Data is on file with the publisher.

ISBN-13: 978–1–60961–516–1 hardcover

Distributed to the trade by Macmillan

2   4   6   8   10   9   7   5   3   1   hardcover

We inspire and enable people to improve their lives and the world around them.
rodalebooks.com

To God, to my family,
and to all the lives that were lost
during the Arab Spring

Although your people live in darkness, they will see a bright light.

Although they live in the shadow of death, a light will shine on them.

MATTHEW 4:16

CONTENTS

Just up from a late practice the night before. Had my driver, Osama, stop for some pizza on the way home. He knows just a few words of English. He knows my name, Alex. He knows come *and* practice *and* bank *and* market. *He knows the pizza place I like, where they make it fresh. He pretty much has all my basic needs covered.*

He's a funny guy, a good guy. Always talking shit about Qaddafi. I can't understand a word he says, but I can tell he's talking shit. It's like he's spitting the word Qaddafi *onto the dashboard in front of him, like it disgusts him to even have the man's name on his lips. Osama's like a lot of the Libyans I've met in the short time I've been here—very expressive. We don't speak the same language, but their body language gives them away. When they are happy, I can tell. When they are angry, I can tell. When they are confused or over-whelmed, I can tell this, too, and with Osama I can tell this most of all. His mood is in his smile, in the way he spits Qaddafi's name from his lips.*

I'd fallen asleep watching a European basketball game, and the television is still on when I wake up. It's a good thing I set the alarm. Without it, I'd be dead asleep. With it, I'm just dead tired. The plan is to hit the gym early, eight forty-five, just me and my coach. I want to stretch, get some shots in, work on a couple of things. We've got a big game this weekend against our rival, Al-Ahly Benghazi. It's like the Celtics and the Lakers when our teams play, only with rocks and soda bottles being thrown onto the court. Last time we played was my first game for Al-Nasr, in a nice arena in Tripoli. Both teams are from Benghazi, but there's so much noise and excitement around these games that they need to put us in a big venue. The fans get into it, and so do the players, even if it's just to avoid the rocks and the soda bot-tles, even if it's a neutral-site game. Either way, it'll be bloody, brutal. I want to be ready. I have not come all this way to play professional basketball in Libya, then sleep through my alarm just because I'm dead tired.

Osama's running late. He's not answering his phone, so I call my coach, Sherif Azmy. Coach Sherif is a local legend, the John Wooden of the Middle East. He's got this reputation for running his players like crazy. He's originally from Egypt, used to play himself. Knows his stuff: fundamentals, Xs and Os, all of that. Learned the game in the States, going around to Five-Star camps and clinics. Guys who play for him say he runs them so hard, it takes a couple of years off their careers, but he knows the game. He plays to win. Treats his players like family. Some, anyway.

Coach Sherif answers his phone like it's already in his hand. He must recognize my number, because he answers in English. He says, "What?" (His English is good, but he doesn't want to wear it out.)

I say, "Coach, it's Alex. I'm still waiting for Osama. I'll be a few minutes late."

He says, "No, no, no. What are you talking about?" Like I'm crazy for even calling. Like I've got no idea what's going on.

I say, "For practice."

He says, "There is no practice, Alex. Don't you see outside?"

I cross to the window to see what he means. My apartment is on the seventh floor, overlooking the main square, the heart of Benghazi. The apartment actually belongs to one of Qaddafi's sons, Mutassim, a lieutenant colonel in the Libyan army. He's cleared out to make room for me for the run of the basketball season. It's furnished with his fine things—beautiful couches with gold trim, a big-screen television, interesting art. He's about ten years older than me, but his tastes seem to come from another time. Still, it's an amazing place. And convenient: two blocks from the arena where we play our home games; two blocks from the Al-Nasr Sporting Club, where we practice and train; one block from a place that reminds me of a Ruby Tuesday, where I take a lot of my meals.

I look out the window at a crowd of protestors on the street below. My view is obstructed by the other buildings, but it appears to be the same crowd from the day before, from the day before that. The same size, the same temper. Mostly men, some military. For four or five days now, there has been unrest. Shots have been fired into the air like exclamation points.

Since December, there has been a wave of protests throughout the Arab world. Demonstrations. Rallies. There has been the sudden overthrow of governments in Tunisia and Egypt. Last week, on what the newspapers are calling the Friday of Departure, Egyptian president Hosni Mubarak announced his resignation, following weeks of mostly civil disobedience. The news set off wild celebrations in the streets of Cairo and across the Middle East. I know this mostly because the pictures from these protests pop up on my home screen every time I go online. I do not know this from looking outside my window, from talking to people. I am too focused on basketball, on my team, to think too long, too hard about anything else.

Even so, the spirit of this Arab uprising is in the air and all around. It is impossible to miss. Here in Benghazi it has been a peaceable movement. That is how it starts: There is a call for change. There is anger and tension, yes, but there is also order and civility . . . for now.

Whatever is happening on the street below, it comes to me through my window like a lot of noise. It is nothing. And yet across the world, through the Internet, news of the protests on the streets of Libya reaches my family in the States like a warning. Just yesterday, before practice, my oldest brother Joseph pleaded with me on Skype to pack my bags and come home. He said, "You have got to get out of there, Alex. It's bad."

I said, "It's nothing. Everything's fine. You'll see."

Today, now, it still feels like nothing—just shouting and chanting and meaningless gunfire. I say as much to Coach Sherif. I say, "This has been going on for four days," I say. "This is nothing new."

He says, "No, Alex, it's turned. They're killing people. Look."

I look and look, but I cannot get a full view through my window, so I tell Coach Sherif I'll call him back. I set the phone down on the kitchen counter, then I open the heavy door to my apartment and take the steps to the roof two at a time. I live on the top floor, so it is only one flight. I have been to the roof almost every day since I arrived in Libya at the end of December. It's where I hang my clothes to dry when I do my wash. It's where I come to unwind, to take in the panorama of my strange new surroundings. From the roof, I can see the main square in front of my building. I can see across to the arena and over to the soccer field where I sometimes do my running. Today I look down and see the full swarm of protestors below—about three hundred people, some of them wearing the deep green of the Libyan flag, pressed up against each other like they are at a concert. They are jumping, shouting, dancing. Almost everyone has a fist in the air in a show of defiance. There seems to be a great too many of them squeezed into a not-so-great, too-tight space.

The protesters all appear to be facing the same direction, looking at the same thing. I follow their gazes to a row of military police wearing white hats with a Libyan-green stripe. They are thirty, forty strong.

They move slowly across the square to fill the space between the police line and the swarm of protesters. My first thought is that the police are only trying to break up the crowd, which has been bottlenecked into this narrow, open space.

My next thought, still, is that this is nothing. There is no evidence of violence. There is only the threat of violence. There is only more of the same. And so after two or three minutes, I race back down the stairs to my apartment, wondering again what's taking Osama so long to get here. Wondering what had Coach Sherif so agitated.

Just . . . wondering.

ONE | LAGOS

THE FIRST TIME I TOUCHED A BASKETBALL I was barefoot on a dirt court, looking up at a square hoop. The hoop was square because it was really a milk crate nailed to a tree. My brothers had cut the bottom from the crate and hung the thing just high enough to be out of reach, but not so high that the oldest of us couldn't maybe dunk on it.

Something to shoot for, you know.

It wasn't even a proper basketball when we were superlittle. We played with a soccer ball. Everybody in Nigeria played soccer, so there was always a ball around somewhere. Hardly anyone played basketball. We lived in a village just outside Lagos, the biggest city in the country, and best I could tell, the only kids who played basketball were me and my brothers. We had our own little court, our own rules. Basically, it was every man for himself: No fouls. No out-of-bounds. Two-on-two, the As versus the Js. It was me and my brother Anthony against my brothers Joseph and Johnson. I was the youngest—probably six or seven—when we started keeping score. We had an older sister, Malinda, and then after me there was another sister, Melissa, and our baby brother, Justin, but it was just the four older boys playing basketball. We went at it all day long. We played to thirty-two by twos. Winners out. We didn't call it *winners out* or *make-it-take-it* or any of those names you hear on the playgrounds in the States. That's just the way we did it.

We kept track of wins. After a while, we'd wipe away the total and start fresh. Joseph and Johnson always had the most wins. They liked to brag about it, hold it over our heads. It wasn't really fair, the way we had the teams split up. Joseph was older and bigger than Anthony. Johnson was older and bigger than me. We were overmatched this way and that. But these were the teams. Johnson, to this day, is probably one of the most gifted athletes I've ever seen. His thing was to move that crate higher and higher on the tree, and he'd spend hours jumping and jumping; when it got to where he could dunk, he'd get out the ladder and move the crate higher still. By the time he was eleven, the crate was ten feet up, and he was dunking like it was nothing at all. At one point, he had a forty-three-inch vertical leap, which was just sick. World-class sick—better than all but a handful of guys playing in the NBA.

Anthony and I couldn't really compete against that kind of size and that kind of talent, so we developed a very physical game. It was a matter of survival. To this day, I'm a very physical player. Also to survive, I spent a lot of time working on my outside shot, because there was no way I could play with those guys above the crate. Joseph and Johnson would dunk on us all day long, and we'd fire up jumpers just to keep the game close. That's probably where I got my shot, because the soccer ball was almost as big as the milk crate. There was no backboard, so you had to have excellent touch. You had to hit it clean. We didn't understand the concept of "nothing but net"—never heard that phrase—but that was basically the idea, because if you tried to bank the ball off the rough of the tree, it would bounce every which way.

I played all out, all the time. I would get my shoulder right in your stomach. I'd go right into your chest. Basically, going up against my older brothers like that, you had to go through them. They were beasts. To get to the crate nailed to the tree, you couldn't go around them. You could only go through them or shoot over them. It helped that we played without fouls, because we fouled each other like mad. From time to time, we'd put it together and find a way to win, but for the most part, Joseph and Johnson just killed us. Every day, they just killed us.

We had a bunch of cousins up and down our street, but they never played. Mostly, it was the four of us, picking apart each other's games, lifting each other's games, beating the crap out of each other on our crappy dirt court. Basketball was becoming more popular in Nigeria at the time, because everyone was following Hakeem Olajuwon. He was also from Lagos. He was the number one pick in the NBA draft the year I was born—the same year Michael Jordan was drafted—so that was a big, big deal. Back then he was known as Akeem, "Akeem the Dream." All the noise and fuss over Hakeem Olajuwon wasn't enough to get everybody to stop playing soccer and switch to basketball, but he was like our local hero. Kids looked up to him—not just because he was tall but because he was one of us. We were drawn to him, each in our own way. It was kind of amazing to see Hakeem Olajuwon play at such a high level, because he was like all the other kids in our village. Growing up, he only played soccer. He was a goal-keeper. He didn't start playing basketball until he was fifteen years old, and even when he made it to the NBA—even when basketball was becoming more and more popular—there was no place for a kid in Lagos to play the sport in any organized way. There were no facilities—no basketballs!—so watching Olajuwon became another something for me and my brothers to shoot for.

Of course, we couldn't watch him play directly. We couldn't get any NBA games on television, but we could follow him in the newspapers. We could listen to our uncles talk about him. We could call out his name on our dirt court and make like we were him. But we couldn't actually *see* Olajuwon play. We could only close our eyes and imagine it. The only basketball we ever got to watch, really, came to us through the VHS tapes my father brought home from his trips to the States. He had a government job, which meant a lot of overseas travel. He didn't know too much about basketball, but he knew we were crazy for it, so he used to bring back these compilation tapes, and my brothers and I would watch those things until we wore them out. Oscar Robertson, Earl Monroe . . . those were the guys I grew up watch-ing, so I tried to pattern my game on theirs. This basically meant that on the one hand, I was forced to be a very physical player—going up against my brothers every day—but on the other hand, I was trying to spin and dish and work all these old-school, vintage moves into my game. It was a weird combination, to try to match the grace and style of those older players to the rough-and-tumble style we were starting to see from guys like Charles Barkley, but that was all I knew.

Bernard King, he was something to see. He was another one of my favorites, another one of my models. From Earl the Pearl I learned to spin, to duck in and out, to play smooth, but my overall game was more like Bernard's. It was a scrappy, tenacious, hard-charging, get-a-shot-off-any-way-you-can sort of approach. You couldn't play Earl's finesse game against a couple of strong Nigerian boys. It just wouldn't work. You had to drop your shoulder. You had to initiate contact. You had to fight for an opening. You had to play it more like Bernard or Charles. You had to find your shot by going through the other guy.

Another weird thing was that we never really had a chance to watch a full-on game until we were older. All we saw were clips, highlights, so we had no idea what it meant to manage the clock, to change the tempo, to figure out a way to turn momentum to advantage. We couldn't understand or appreciate any of those battles you sometimes see in a game: two guys going at each other every possession, two guys giving as good as they're getting. Larry Bird versus Magic Johnson. Hakeem Olajuwon versus Patrick Ewing. All of that stuff you pick up just by osmosis, just by watch-ing game after game after game—that was all lost to us as kids. We only knew what it meant to go to the rim—hard. To drain a three. To find the open man with a no-look pass. The back-and-forth, the rhythm of the game—all of that would come later.

Much, much later.

———❧———

When I write that we had a bunch of cousins living up and down our street, I don't mean to be vague: There were too many of us to count. My father, Joseph Owumi, is one of sixty-seven children.

Sixty-seven! He was actually one of the babies of his family—the sixty-first in line. His father—my grandfather—had twenty-three wives, and they all lived in the same village, on the same compound. There were, like, twenty houses all lined up, all looking pretty much the same, and each one was filled with aunts and uncles and cousins. My grandfather owned a lot of land, raised a lot of cattle, and he was considered a rich, rich man. He had to be, I guess, to support twenty-three wives. The way it worked in Nigeria was that if you could take care of twenty-three women, you could marry twenty-three women, and even though the total sum of my grandfather's wealth must have been considerable, we all lived simply. There wasn't *that* much to go around.

My grandfather and most of his children were landowners or farmers. They worked hard. We grew a lot of corn, but we also raised and sold a lot of cattle. My father, too; he worked the land when he wasn't traveling. We didn't have a lot, but we had enough. When I was a little kid, I was put to work herding goats, herding cows. When my turn came around, I'd have to go with my father to slaughter one of our cows. He taught us all how to do this, one by one, and the way he did it was a two-man job. One person would hold the cow and keep it still, and the other would cut its throat, but not before we said a little blessing for the cow. There was a whole ceremony attached to the ritual, because the cow was going to feed three or four of our families, and we needed to honor the animal and give thanks.

I can still remember the very first time it was my turn to cut the throat. It was like a rite of passage. I was about six years old. I was with my father and one of my uncles. My father showed me where to make the cut. He said, "You cannot be soft about it, Alex. You cannot do it halfway."

A cow's skin is very tough. I learned that under the neck is the softest skin, the easiest to pierce. You know how when you see an aggressive bull or a big, fat cow, there's always a low-hanging bit of skin beneath the neck that's kind of droopy? That's where the skin is most tender, so that's where you want to make your first cut. With a pig, you're supposed to go in under the front legs but with a cow you go right under the throat, and what I recall most about that first time is the blood. Oh, man, there was so much blood. It just came pouring out, like a waterfall, but I tried to be a big man about it. That was always the goal: to be just like my father, just like our uncles. We did not complain. We did not shrink from our chores. We did what we were told.

I was soaked through with blood, and it took a long time for me to wash it all away. We did not have plumbing back then—that would not come for a few more years—so we had to go to the well and fetch a heavy pail of water and scrub ourselves clean. Always, you could look out across our compound and spot some cousin or other hauling water or bathing outside. Sometimes we bathed in the house, but it was easier outside. When we lived in an apartment, nobody wanted to haul that bucket of water up the stairs.

We were a big extended family. A lot of us lived in houses up and down the same street; some of us lived in the same apartment buildings. We shopped at the same market. We were born in the same hospital. And on Sundays, we all went to the same church— Christ the King. It wasn't a traditional church like you see in America. There were no pillars or spires, no vaulted ceilings or stained glass windows. It was just a plain, nothing-special brick building—for a long time, it wasn't even finished—but we packed that place on Sunday mornings. We'd gather to listen to Father Felix Ojimba do his thing, and then I'd stay on with my siblings for Sunday school while our parents and grandparents and aunts and uncles got together for a family visit. It was the centerpiece of our week—each week, without fail. And all week long, our parents kept on us to say our prayers, to mind our chores, to follow the teachings of the Bible.

This wasn't so unusual where we lived. The extended Owumi clan wasn't the only Catholic family in Lagos. In fact, the southern part of Nigeria where we lived was predominantly Catholic. In the north there were a lot of Muslims, and this led to a lot of conflict and tension, but where we were, we were just like everybody else. Where we were, you went to church, you went to Sunday school, you said your prayers and counted your blessings. You considered Father Felix to be like family—and he was, in a deep and fundamental way. For a time in there, my brother Johnson even wanted to be a bishop—that's how connected we were to the church in our house—but that only lasted until he discovered girls. Actually, until he discovered one girl in particular, and she became his wife. That was the end of Johnson's spiritual ambitions.

We all went to the same school, too, down the road from where we lived. And school, for me and my siblings, for all of us cousins, was extremely important. It mattered most of all. In Nigeria, folks take school pretty seriously. The school day is longer than it is in the States and in some other parts of the world. We went from seven o'clock in the morning until six o'clock at night. There was a big emphasis on math and science, and we all took to it in one way or another, to where a great many of my cousins left for college in the United States at fifteen or sixteen years old. My father, too, left Nigeria at about the same age to go to university.

I never knew my paternal grandfather—he died when my father was still a boy—but he certainly left his mark. He was not only rich, he was also the chief of our village, and in that part of the world, this was like being royalty. My father and all of his brothers were princes. When my brothers and I were born, we were princes, too. Even today, if I go back to Nigeria, I am greeted as Prince Alexander. There's a military detail that follows us around, almost like the Secret Service. It's wild, but it's just how it is. My father eventually became a chief, and so did my brother Joseph, and one day when I get married, I'll go back and become a chief as well—another rite of passage. There's an elaborate ceremony. The entire village comes together to anoint the new chiefs, who are dressed out in beautiful costumes and scented with special powders and oils. It's almost primal, like a throwback to another time and place, and yet it's a part of my family. It's who we are. And when my turn comes, I'll wear all that finery and hole up in our house for seven days, receiving visitors, and take part in that ritual, same as my father and brothers, same as my uncles, same as my grandfather.

I did know my paternal grandmother. She was like a beacon in our lives. She did not come with my family when we eventually moved to the United States. She stayed behind and became a kind of godmother to the whole community. She was ninety-eight years old when she died, and I remember her as a tough old bird. Everyone looked up to her, sought her out for advice, and looked to her for approval. My father and uncles built her a great big house in the middle of the village, and that's where she held forth for the rest of her days. In fact, that's where she's buried, right next to my grandfather, and when she died, I remember feeling like a light had gone out in our family. The ways we lived, the ways we grew up—it would be hard for us to see or know those ways again.

My mother could never have known what she was getting into, marrying a Nigerian prince. You couldn't tell by looking at my father as a young man, by the way he carried himself, that he was royalty. He dressed cheaply in mismatched clothes. His English was terrible. He did not look like royalty any more than someone who stacks groceries or delivers packages or drives a cab looks like royalty.

Here is how they met: My mother, Claudia, was born and raised in Cambridge, Massachusetts. She went to school at Lesley University, which was also in Cambridge. My father was studying finance at a school called Boston State, which is now known as UMass Boston. My mother's roommate happened to be dating my father's roommate, so I guess it was inevitable that my parents would meet. One day my mother went up to my father's apartment to collect her friend, and my father answered the door. He was wearing one of the ugliest sweaters my mother had ever seen, and she tried not to laugh. She knew that if she laughed, she would not be able to explain herself, because my father could hardly understand a word she said.

Despite their many differences, they fell in love and started a family, and it wasn't until some years later that the full scope of my father's royalty became clear to my mother. He didn't talk about it because he didn't believe it was relevant here in America. Here in America, he was just like any other immigrant seeking a good education, a meaningful career. My mother knew he was from a big family, but I do not think she knew *how* big, exactly. After a while, she came to know that he was from an important family, but she didn't know *how* important. The story only emerged in bits and pieces, and when my parents decided to return to Nigeria to raise their family, that's when two and two started to add up to sixty-seven. That's when she knew.

My mother was like a fish out of water in Nigeria. She was fairly light skinned—her father was black, and her mother was Portuguese. She made for an odd picture against the rest of our large family. Folks in Lagos, they looked at my mother like she was white. When she first got there, she couldn't speak the language. We spoke Urhobo in our village. There's really no national language in Nigeria. The "official" language is actually English, but that's only because there are so many different languages and dialects that English is the only real common denominator. There's Urhobo, there's Hausa. There's the Yoruba tribe, the Igbo tribe. Some of the dialects are close enough that if you understand one you can understand the other, but it is difficult to read or study in one if it isn't your native tongue. Urhobo is a difficult language, but my mother picked it up quickly, and it wasn't long before she was almost fluent. If it weren't for her light, light skin, you might have thought she'd been born there.

She spoke English to us in the home, and we studied English in school as well—but in truth, our English was as terrible as our father's had been. It was passable at best. We could understand words and phrases. We could make ourselves understood. But we couldn't read or think or study in English.

We could only close our eyes and imagine.

My mother spoke Urhobo well enough that she was able to

work in the local schools. Eventually, she became the principal of the International Embassy School in Nigeria, which was a whole lot nicer than the schools we attended as kids. Our elementary school was pretty harsh. At our school, the teachers used to beat the students if they were late to class or if they came to class unprepared. It was brutal. They'd take you in the back and lash you with a switch. We Owumis were never beaten, though— partly because our parents saw to it that we were never late or unprepared but also because of our stature in the community. After all, we were royalty, but even more than that, my father was active in local politics and had many important connections, and my mother was a local educator with many connections as well.

Every afternoon, when our school day was finally done, we'd go from our school to the embassy school to wait for my mother to finish work. We'd hang back and watch all the British kids with all of their fancy clothes and manners. There'd be American kids, too, and my brothers and I used to fantasize that maybe we could go to this school and fit ourselves in. It was like our window into the wide, wide world. All we knew about life beyond Nigeria was what we could learn from the VHS tapes and books and occasional copies of *Sports Illustrated* my father brought home from his travels, what we could pick up in the halls of my mother's school. We were forced by our circumstances to become good students of human behavior, because there was no other way for us to learn. We didn't go to the movies. We didn't watch a lot of television. We only had the public access channels, which didn't come on until four o'clock in the afternoon. There was no cable television where we lived. Only the richest people in Nigeria had satellite television—and in those days, the satellite dishes were huge, the size of a swimming pool! Cartoons came on at four o'clock, and after that there'd be news, and I remember half listening, half watching as my parents tuned in, trying to understand how the world worked beyond our village. In this way, I learned the names of our neighboring African countries. I learned about our president, General Ibrahim Babangida, who came to power about a year or so after I was born by overthrowing the government of Major General Muhammadu Buhari. I learned about Nelson Mandela. I learned about Colonel Muammar Qaddafi, whom my brothers and I thought of as a savior. Mandela and Qaddafi were like heroes to us, the same way Hakeem Olajuwon was a hero to us. We did not listen between the lines of what was said on the news. We only listened to the headline, and the message that came across was that the Libyan government under Qaddafi was doing many good things for its poor African neighbors. They were sending a lot of money to Nigeria, Sudan, Niger. They were helping people throughout the region.

Colonel Qaddafi was not known in our village as a tyrant. In fact, people looked up to him. He was respected, revered. There was evidence of his good works all across the continent. He was known as the king of kings.

If you'd taken me aside and told me I'd one day play basketball for this man, for a team run by his family—the royal family of the king of kings—I would have thought it'd be pretty cool. I would have thought it'd be an honor.

I do not mean to suggest that I was overly ambitious or overly determined to understand the world around me. I was only trying to understand how we Owumis fit into the bigger picture, because by the time I was eight or nine, I started to hear my parents talk more and more about moving to the United States. This was a thrilling prospect for me and my siblings. We did not know much about life in America. We only knew what we'd read in books like *The Adventures of Tom Sawyer* that my father would bring home for us, along with our precious NBA tapes. We also knew that our oldest sister, Malinda, wanted to go to school there and that my mother was anxious to return home. My father was being considered for a number of jobs there, as well. Underneath all of this talk, it was clear to all of us that my father was having many successes at work. He was able to build us a bigger house with indoor plumbing. He was able to build a house for his mother. And yet, even with our bigger house, we lived in the same simple ways. I still wore my brothers' hand-me-down clothes, and by the time they were handed down to me, they were looking pretty shabby.

But I didn't care how I dressed. When I wasn't in school, I was running around shirtless with my brothers on our dirt court. All we cared about, really, was basketball. The more we played, the more we watched those NBA highlights, the more we imagined ourselves playing on a real team on a real court with a real basketball. I finally got a pair of sneakers when I was seven years old, and that was a great, great moment. We all knew about Air Jordans, but these were a no-name brand, with a Velcro strap instead of laces. Even so, my brothers and I wore our new shoes as a point of pride. And they came just in time, because we were starting to hurt ourselves playing in our bare feet. The bigger we got, the more weight we carried. You'd step on a rock here and there. You'd turn an ankle or scratch the bottoms of your feet or land in just the wrong way. Once I stepped on a nail and it went all the way through my foot, from the bottom all the way to the top. It hurt like you wouldn't believe, and it also hurt to look at. One of my brothers pulled it out for me—just yanked the nail right out—and I had to go to the hospital to get the wound patched up, but the very next day, I was back out there playing.

The sneakers were a game changer, and they came at a time when my older brothers were having their growth spurts and it was starting to seem like we could maybe play the game for real. As we grew, we were all hoping we'd get our height from our mother's side of the family. Her brothers are six-nine, six-six, six-four. My Uncle Clifford is the shortest at six-two. They all played basketball growing up. A couple of them even played in college, so my mother knew the game. She used to come out and watch us play on our dirt court and show us what we were doing wrong. She knew the correct way to shoot, the correct way to dribble. One thing about basketball: If you don't grow up playing it—if you don't hang around the game and soak in the movements, the gestures, the nods and feints—you'll never look like a natural. With a player like Hakeem Olajuwon, who came to the game late, there was always something off about the way he handled the ball—like he wasn't born to it, you know. As great as he was, as proficient as he was, when he stepped to the line to take a foul shot, I always felt like he was still getting familiar with the ball. When he put the ball on the floor, it's like he was still developing his handle. There was something precise and studied about how he moved with the ball, compared to the innate, natural way most great players did their thing. And that's what my mother used to see when she came out to watch us play. As much time as we spent out there on our little dirt court—as athletic and physical and competitive as we all were—the game was still foreign to us. Yeah, it was first and foremost. Yeah, it was in our faces. But at the same time, it was just out of reach. It could be something small that she'd pick out and tell us to work on. Like dribbling with our heads down. Like shooting with our arms, from our hips instead of with our wrists, from up high. Like giving up our dribble before we knew what would happen next. In the beginning, she was the one who taught us the basic rules—double dribbling, traveling—and so she set us straight.

We probably got our athleticism from my father. He was a tremendous soccer player—just a phenomenal athlete. His brothers, too. Two of my uncles played on the Nigerian national team, back in the day when Pelé was still playing on the international scene. They were always trying to get my father to play with them, but he never thought he had time for organized soccer. He was too busy studying, trying to make something of himself, but his footwork was just unreal.

Like my mother, he'd come out to watch us play, but he didn't really understand the game. He couldn't even act as referee. The only time he'd step in and say anything was if one of us was punching another one of us in the face. That kind of thing had no place in sports, he used to say. Other than that, he just let us play. He'd stand and watch with his arms folded, shaking his head. I could be on the ground, with blood coming out of my mouth from one of Joseph's or Johnson's elbows, and I'd look at my father as if to say "Are you gonna help me here?" And he would just shake his head and say, "Get up out of the dirt, Alex."

So I would.

—ᴍ—

One day, when I was about nine, my parents told us we were moving to the United States. It did not come as a surprise. The only surprise was when they told us we would first be making a stop in London on our way to America. We had family there, and it was decided that we would stay with them for a period of time. I did not care so much where we were going, only that we were going. It's not that I didn't love our village, our school, and our big, big family, but I was ready for something new. I had never been beyond Lagos, so what did it matter if we went to London or New York or Boston? Wherever we went, it would be an adventure.

We did not know what to expect in London, only that we would be visiting our aunts and uncles and cousins. What I remember most of all is that it was very cold. I had never been so cold in my life. Also, I had never seen so many white faces. So many blonde and blue-eyed women! I was old enough to appreciate the beautiful Nigerian women back home, but this was a different kind of beauty. This was exotic and strange and wonderful. It was such a culture shock, but it was a good kind of culture shock. The language, too, was a surprise. The English that was spoken on the streets of London sounded nothing like the English we spoke in our house or in our classrooms back home. I wanted to slow everyone down so I could understand, so I could make myself understood as well, but the way I dealt with this new language barrier was to not even bother. I became suddenly and impossibly shy. I had never been a shy kid, but in London, I wouldn't talk to anyone other than my brothers and sisters and cousins.

The only time I was my outgoing self was on the basketball court, and this was a whole other revelation. We still didn't own a basketball, but once we got to London, we started playing with a real ball, shooting at a real hoop attached to a real backboard. It took me and my brothers a while to adjust to these new surroundings. We were used to playing our own way. We even caught a bunch of shit the first couple of days because we didn't wear socks inside our sneakers. After all those years playing barefoot, we'd gotten into the habit of slipping our feet directly into our sneakers. That's all we knew. That's how we were comfortable. But then we got to London, and all these British kids started goofing on us like we'd just stepped out of the jungle.

They stopped goofing, though, once they saw us play. Our games stacked up just fine. Physically, athletically, these other kids couldn't touch us, even though we clearly needed to work on our fundamentals. Right away, I could see that I'd be one of the stronger players in my age-group, but I played a little bit rough. Once we started playing organized games, I'd foul out right away. I was way too aggressive—so aggressive that some of these kids didn't even want to let me play. I'd just drop my shoulder and barrel into people the same way I went up against my brothers back home, only here it wasn't really appreciated.

I had some trouble adjusting to a real ball, too. In a lot of ways, it was an easy adjustment, because the ball was dimpled and you could get a good grip on it, but it was also bigger than a soccer ball, and heavier. For years and years, I'd gotten familiar with a small ball, so I wasn't so sure of myself at first. Over time, I came to realize that spending all that time with a smaller ball actually helped my handle, because it allowed me to do a whole bunch of things when my hands were way too small to even think about making those kinds of moves with a regulation ball. Still, I was a little clumsy making the transition.

Another big adjustment was the backboard, which I tried to work into my game straightaway. These days, I've got a real knack for shooting it off the glass—not quite like Dwyane Wade, who's probably got the best bank shot in the game today—but I've learned to mix it up. I've learned that it's best to hit it clean—*nothing but net!*—but the backboard can bail you out of a tough spot.

Mostly, though, I tried to fit myself into the concept of a team game, which was another new thing for me. In London, there were a ton of kids who played. It wasn't just me and my brothers going at it hard, playing two-on-two over and over until the sun went down. Playing to thirty-two by twos, and then starting over again.

No, this was me and my brothers and cousins, fitting ourselves into a game and a culture that was way beyond our experience.

This was me with a whole new something to shoot for.

I am back in my apartment, scrambling to catch my breath, my bearings. I try to get Coach Sherif on the phone, but the call won't go through.

I try again.

Nothing.

Through my window, I can hear the commotion in the square below. The noise, the shouting—it sounds like it's getting louder, bigger. Like a great wave about to crash, like something huge is about to happen. Whatever it is, I don't want to miss it. I don't want to be stuck inside, so I grab a bottle of water and again climb the stairs to the roof.

I've only been gone a couple of minutes, but in that time military police have closed in on the crowd. They are squeezing the protesters into a kind of standoff. There is no place for the police to go but through the protesters. There is no place for the protesters to go but up against each other. It feels to me like a rubber band about to snap. From up here looking down, one hundred feet in the air, the movements on each side look like they've been choreographed, rehearsed. I cannot imagine what will happen. I can only wish this moment away, so that the streets will clear and I can make my way to practice. This is my main concern just now. This is my priority: for life to return to normal.

I take a sip of water, and as I bring the bottle to my lips, I see a flash of movement from the corner of the scene. For the first time, I notice a vehicle. Perhaps it has been there all along, but I am only now seeing it. From this height, from this distance, it does not appear to be an official vehicle, but it has emerged in the thick of the crowd as if from nowhere. I've got no idea how I missed it, if I even did, but there it is.

The crowd on the police side of the standoff has seemed to swallow up the vehicle, surrounded it, and out of that crowd there emerges a man dressed in military greens. He climbs onto the roof of the vehicle— some kind of truck or SUV—followed by another man who does the same, and as they position themselves, I see there is a gun of some kind mounted to the roof as well, possibly a rifle. From this distance it is difficult to tell, but from the body language of the two men, it is clear they are getting ready to shoot into the crowd.

And they are. They do. Before I can make sense of what I'm seeing, the first man starts firing and firing, while the second man starts feeding him ammunition. They are working together like they have done this before, many times before, like their movements have been practiced. It is like something out of a movie, only it is not a movie. It is like a bad cliché, only it is not a cliché. I do not wish to watch, but I cannot look away. The sound of the rapid fire reaches me on the roof, and along with it I can see dozens of protesters drop to their knees, knocked to the ground, stumbling and staggering to oblivion. Oh, my God, it's just crazy. Sick and terrible and crazy. Within seconds, there is blood and fear and mayhem, all over. The crowd seems to want to disperse, but there is nowhere for this mass of people to turn. They are trapped, helpless.

Everywhere I look, people are running. There is nowhere for them to run, but they are running just the same. As they move, they are gunned down. As they stand still, they are gunned down. As they are thrown up against each other, desperate for escape, they are gunned down.

What I am seeing makes no sense. It does not attach itself to the situation I have seen outside my building for the past few days, to the Libya I have come to know in the few weeks I have been here playing professional basketball. It does not fit with the pictures that have been popping up on my home screen, with what I've been reading on the Internet, what I've been discussing in broken English with my teammates.

A thing like this, it doesn't happen right in front of you. Right in front of me.

A thing like this, I cannot tell the good guys from the bad guys. I cannot pick sides.

A thing like this . . . what is it, exactly? I have no frame of reference for what I'm seeing, but it becomes clear soon enough. I fix on a group of young men about twenty feet in front of the armed vehicle. I am drawn to the shouting of one young man in particular. I cannot make out what he is saying, only that he is trying to stir up the other young protesters around him. I try to read his expression from my perch seven stories above him, and just as my eyes begin to take him in, I hear another volley of shots—rat-a-tat-a-tat!—and see the young man thrown back against the crowd. He falls to the street, clutching his side. One moment he is standing, shouting, and the next he is recoiling, rolling on the ground in pain.

It occurs to me that soon—very soon—this young man will be dead. He stops moving, and I think that perhaps he is dead already.

As I watch this horrifying scene unfold, the bottle of water drops from my hand and falls to the tar-and-gravel roof. I imagine my jaw drops as well. It is astonishing, what I am seeing. It is unknowable.

Suddenly my legs buckle. I can no longer stand, so I drop to the floor of the roof, too. I do not know why. I do not know if I am weak at the knees, sickened by the massacre on the street, or if I am trying to get low, to safety, moving by some survival instinct. As far as I know, I am not in the line of fire. There is no military presence on the rooftops surrounding the square—none that I can see. But I am flat on the ground, the side of my face pressed onto the roof's rough surface, as if I'm trying to press myself down into the safety of my apartment below.

Finally, mercifully, the shooting stops. Or at least I can no longer hear it up on the roof. I can only hear yelling and screaming. I can only hear crying. If I could understand Arabic, I could make some sense of the yelling and screaming, but I can only make out the fear and confusion and madness.

I scramble to my knees and to my feet. I stand and take a final look at the square before retreating back into the building, back to my apartment. I reach again for my cell phone, but I can't get it to work. I fumble for my laptop to see if I can maybe connect to Skype, maybe reach my girlfriend, my parents, my brothers or sisters back home, but the Internet is down.

I do not know what to do. Really, I have no idea. My head is a mess with images I'll never shake. I cannot think.

I keep pressing the redial button on my cell phone. Over and over, I keep doing this. Finally, after sixteen, seventeen tries, the call goes through.

Coach Sherif answers, again immediately. He says, "Alex? Alex, are you okay?"

I say, "Coach, they're gunning people down. Right on the street, right outside my building. Like, dozens and dozens of people."

He says, "It is what I told you. It is not safe."

There is nothing to say to this, so I wait for my coach to finish his thought.

He says, "I am on my way to Egypt."

I do not think I have heard him correctly, but then I think about it. Coach Sherif is Egyptian—of course he is on his way to Egypt. The thought makes me furious. And afraid. The whole time I was up on the roof—maybe ten minutes, maybe twenty—he was arranging for his escape.

I say, "What about me? What the hell am I supposed to do?"

Later, I will realize that it would have been impossible for my coach or the team president or anyone from the Al-Nasr Benghazi office to get to me, but in the moment I can only fume and curse. I'm pissed that I have been left behind. I'm scared out of my mind.

He says, "We will try to send somebody for you, Alex. Stay calm. Someone will come for you soon."

This is bullshit, I know. This is just a way for Coach Sherif to get himself off the phone and to clear his conscience. Nobody will come into the middle of what appears to be a war zone, just to get me out.

The call is dropped, and I am alone. There is nothing to do but stand and pace and worry. I try calling home, but I cannot get through. I fall into a weird trance, dialing and redialing. I try to call my girlfriend, my parents, my siblings. Over and over, I keep dialing, and I stare and stare at the display on the phone, willing the calls to go through. Each time, the message comes back the same:

"Call failed."

"Call failed."

"Call failed."

TWO | BOSTON

BASKETBALL WAS WAITING for us in the United States.

So was my father.

He'd left London a couple of months ahead of us for a job as a professor of finance and strategic studies at Harvard University. He had to be there at the start of the fall semester, and I don't think my mom had it together to move the rest of us just yet, so we joined him soon after. He came to meet us at Logan Airport in Boston, and while we were waiting by the baggage claim area, he called me and my brothers over to him.

"See that man over there?" he said, pointing to an extremely tall, extremely well-dressed black man.

We all nodded.

"That's Rick Fox," he said excitedly.

We didn't know who Rick Fox was exactly, but we assumed he was a basketball player. I mean, he looked like an athlete, and he stood a head taller than anyone else in the terminal. What else could we think?

Apparently, while my father had been settling in to his new

job, he started watching basketball—lots and lots of basketball. It was a way for him to both keep connected to his boys back in London and connect with his new community. I wouldn't go so far as to say he'd become a fan, but he was now a student of the game, and one thing about my father, he took his studies seriously. He was proud to be able to tell us the names of all the Celtics players and to fill us in on how the team was doing. We knew Robert Parish, of course, but Larry Bird was no longer playing, and the rest of the lineup was kind of new to us, so he had us beat. Even though we'd never heard of Rick Fox until just this moment, we were thrilled to be standing so close to an actual NBA basketball player—and just as thrilled that our dad had set it up for us. It was a cool, welcome-to-America kind of scene, and we took it as a sign that basketball would hold the same place of importance for us here in Boston as it had back home. At least that's how it registered for me.

Rick Fox was good enough to pose for a family photo. My father had one of those old Polaroid cameras, and we all gathered around, and as I waited for the thing to develop, I thought, *Man, this guy is really tall*. (He was six-seven.) It felt like I was standing beneath a great big tree, and for years I'd take out that picture and show it to my friends and tell them more than they probably wanted to know about my new favorite player. I made it sound like he was an old family friend.

We moved into my grandparents' house on Rindge Avenue in Cambridge—the same house my mother had grown up in. One of the reasons we came back was so she could help out with her folks. Her mother, my grandmother Marguerite, was struggling with Alzheimer's disease and living in a nursing home. We didn't really know her, but this made me incredibly sad. My mother's father, my grandfather William, was on his own for the first time in a big old house. This was also sad.

He was actually a very interesting man, my grandfather. He played a big part in my growing up, just by his example. He'd lived a fascinating life, a meaningful life. He was a staff sergeant during World War II, and after that he went on to become one of the first black golfers to ever play in a PGA event. It happened at Franklin Park in Dorchester, one of the oldest public golf courses in the country. He wasn't the first black golfer to compete on that course, but in a city like Boston, which was one of the slowest cities to integrate (at least in terms of professional sports), it caused a lot of tension and controversy, and I used to sit for hours with my grandfather and listen to his stories about what it took to stand up and be counted.

Soon after we arrived in town, someone at Harvard gave my father tickets to a game at the Boston Garden. This was a huge, huge moment in our lives, because those Celtics games were always sold out. Our seats weren't great—we were in the nosebleed section—but we were in the building. Our buddy Rick Fox was right there on the Garden's famous parquet floor with Dee Brown, Kevin Gamble, and Robert Parish. The Celtics weren't having such a great season, but they were coming off a tremendous run at the top of the league, so there was still a lot of excitement around the team. My brothers and I all knew our Celtics history. We knew about Bill Russell and John Havlicek, Red Auerbach and Bob Cousy. We knew about Bird and Dennis Johnson and Kevin McHale. And, of course, we knew about the tragedy the summer before, when Reggie Lewis, who figured to be the team's next franchise player, collapsed and died of a heart attack during practice.

As we watched this current group of Celtics players, we could see this was a whole other way of playing basketball. They were facing the Atlanta Hawks, and at some point in the first quarter, Dominique Wilkins came flying through the lane and threw down one of his trademark spinning dunks. It was unlike anything I'd ever seen. All I could think was *Wow!* Even from the nosebleed seats, I could feel the energy down on the court. I could feel it in my bones that this was a different brand of basketball than my man Earl the Pearl used to play, than I was used to playing with my brothers. The pace of the game was slower on those old VHS tapes we'd watched from the 1970s and 1980s. Players back then moved around on the floor with purpose, with precision, almost like they were taking their time, picking their spots. This was something completely *other*, you know. This was full tilt, full speed, and maybe the contrast was so stark because it was right there in front of me. Maybe the players were bigger, faster, stronger. Whatever it was, seeing the game live was nothing like watching those old highlight tapes or watching games on television.

And I was hooked. Man, was I hooked.

School was tough, though. My mother enrolled me as a sixth grader at Tobin, a K–8 school down the street from our house. I was still only nine years old, but by her math, by her estimation, this was where I belonged. Remember, I'd had so many more classroom hours than most American kids had, with those ridiculously long school days back home, and I'd gone through so much extra material that this probably made sense. Plus, they'd made me take a bunch of tests, and this was where I'd placed. But after a couple of weeks, the school administrators said they had a different idea. It didn't matter where I was academically, they said. It didn't matter how much extra schooling I'd had in Nigeria. It only mattered how old I was, so they bounced me back to fourth grade with the other kids my age. It wouldn't have been so bad, I don't think, except that I had to switch from the middle school hallway to the elementary school hallway. To this day I don't know why it took the folks in charge so long to figure this one out, but that's how it went down—and for the rest of my time in that school, I was dissed pretty hard about this.

Think about it: to show up at a new school in the sixth grade and then be sent all the way back down to the *fourth* grade—that's something that sticks.

Another tough adjustment was the weather. I know I wrote earlier that we'd never been so cold as we were during our short time in London, but that was nothing compared to our first New England winter. I knew about snow only in theory. I'd seen pictures. I knew you could make snowmen and snowballs and play around in the stuff. What I didn't know—what none of my brothers knew, apparently—was that you had to wear gloves. We went outside on the morning of our first snowfall and starting romping around. A couple of snowballs in, my hands really started to hurt, which was about what I should have expected. First they went numb, and then there was this thick, heavy pain. I started to cry. It felt to me like my hands were about to fall off, and on top of that, they were all scratched and scraped because it wasn't a fine, powdery snow; it was more icy and choppy. So I freaked out a little bit, but that's how different we were, how out of our element.

Really, we didn't know shit about anything.

Meanwhile, we kept playing ball. I think it was around this time that we actually owned our first basketball, which meant we could hit the playgrounds with it anytime we wanted. Our first Christmas in the States, a basketball was what we all wanted to see under the tree. With our own ball, we didn't have to wait for another game to start up that we could maybe join; we could just play and play and play. At first my brothers and I would all hit the court together, like a package deal, but after that first winter, when it started to get a little warmer outside, we'd splinter off into our own separate games. Makes sense, right? By now my brothers were way bigger than me, so we didn't really belong on the same court—Joseph and Anthony, especially. Joseph wasn't especially tall, but as the oldest, he was much more developed physically; he could throw his weight and experience around in a way I couldn't. Johnson and I were close enough in age that we could run together, but after a while, we started playing in leagues and tournaments, so we didn't always match up.

I was actually recruited for my first real team—sort of. Here's that story: I was playing pickup one day, and some guy came over to check me out. I was twelve years old, and this guy was watching me closely. This alone wasn't so unusual, because there were a lot of older guys hanging around the courts where we played. Sometimes they'd run with us; sometimes they'd just watch. This one just watched. He walked over to me when we stopped for a break and said, "Where do you play?"

I wasn't sure I understood the question. I said, "I play right here. Mostly here."

The guy looked at me funny and said, "No, your real team. Where do you *play?*"

So I told him I didn't play any kind of organized ball, and he started telling me about this team I should try to join. Said I'd fit right in. Said it would be good for my game. Said his buddy was the coach and that they were playing in a tournament that weekend, a tournament his buddy also organized, so my brothers took me over to the gym where the team was practicing. I had no idea what to expect. I don't know if the guy called his buddy to tell him I'd be coming over or if I just dropped in cold. Either way, it's like the whole gym pressed PAUSE the moment I walked in the door. The kids on the court just kind of stopped what they were doing and checked me out, each one of them flashing me one of those *Who the hell is this kid?* looks. Like I was fresh meat. These kids were my age, or just about, but they were flying all over the court. Tapping the glass hard. Dunking, some of them. Doing their NBA-type moves.

Talented—like, beyond belief.

Right away, I felt sick to my stomach. Right away, I thought the guy who'd sent me had made a mistake. It was like the mini, pint-size version of what I saw on that first trip to the Boston Garden, with Dominique Wilkins human-highlight-reeling his way to the hoop. I'd never seen anything like this from kids my own age. There was no way I could play with this group. I don't think I'd ever felt intimidated or overwhelmed on a basketball court in my life before, especially by kids my own age, but here I just kind of froze. Here I thought maybe I was a good player for Lagos or London, but that's it.

The team was coached by Al McClain. Everyone knew Al as Ski or Alski—that is, everyone in and around basketball in the Boston area. He'd had a great collegiate career at the University of

New Hampshire; he never made it to the pros, but he'd been drafted by the Houston Rockets in 1984, and he ran this pretty famous local tournament that attracted some of the top players in the country. Folks all over town knew Ski, then and still. To this day, he doesn't drive a car, just rides around Boston on his bicycle.

Ski blew the whistle to get his players moving again, and once they were back to their scrimmage, he walked over to me and my brothers. He looked at me and said, "So you're the one I'm supposed to see."

I stood with him a while, watching these other kids play, and every time I'd see something unreal, Ski would lean in and whisper something about that player. He'd say, "He's the best twelve-year-old in the city." Or "His brother's being recruited by St. John's." I was only standing there for a couple of minutes before I became convinced I was in way over my head, but I eventually made my way onto the court and played okay. Not great, but okay, which meant I was still feeling anxious when I went to play my first game. I didn't start, of course. These kids had been playing together for a while, and Ski didn't really know what I could do, but the very first time he put me into the game, I was just out of my head. The first six shots I took were all threes, and I sank them all. It was crazy—just, you know, one of these times when I was really feeling it. And it made an impression, I'll say that. Ski was known as one of the best shooters in the area, and if you played for him, you had to have an outside game, so this was a great introduction.

And get this: As soon as folks found out my name was Alex, they started calling me Little Alski. A couple of people thought I was the coach's son. They said, "Where'd you find him, Alski? That your kid?"

Alski laughed and said, "No, but he sure shoots like me."

Little Alski. That was my new name.

By the time I got to school the following Monday, the other kids were talking about it. The whole time I'd been there, nobody'd really talked to me. I'd been shy in London, and in Boston I'd become supershy. Getting bounced back those couple of grades didn't help, either, but all of a sudden kids started coming up to me to talk basketball. Kids who weren't even at the tournament. They'd call me by my new nickname. They'd say, "I hear you're pretty good." They'd say, "Man, I heard you tore it up at Alski's tournament." They'd say, "Where you from?"

I'd tell them I was from Nigeria, and they'd look at me kind of funny—probably because they'd never heard of Nigeria. I liked that these kids were talking to me. I was still shy, and I still struggled with my English, but I was also tall and I could play, so I let my game do my talking. From this one game, I got a whole lot of confidence, and it grew and grew. And it wasn't just that game. There was also a three-point shooting contest as part of the tournament, and I lit it up there, too. I think I hit twenty-seven out of thirty in the first round, and I was supposed to go back the next day for the final round, but I never made it. What happened was my report card came in the mail and I'd gotten a B minus in math. The rest of the report card was all As, but in our house we were expected to get straight As, so my father sat me down and told me what's what. He said, "You can do better, Alex."

That first game of the tournament, that first round of the contest, was on a Saturday, and when I got home that afternoon, that's when my father sat me down to talk about my report card. I guess it had come that afternoon in the mail. He wasn't too happy about that one B minus, not at all. To make sure I got the message, he told me I had to stay home the next day and work on my studies. He didn't care that I had to catch a bus to get down to the contest, that I'd made it to the finals. He didn't care that I was finally coming out of my little shell and making my own way with these kids.

(Well, that's probably not a fair thing for me to say. I'm sure my father *cared*. He wanted me to be happy, successful; he wanted me to fit in. But he also wanted me to understand the importance of school. He wanted me to take the same pride in my education as I was now taking in basketball—and this was the way he knew to get his point across.)

By this point, we'd moved out of my grandparents' house in Cambridge and into a place of our own in Dorchester, in downtown Boston. It was a nice house, a nice neighborhood, only it didn't feel so nice to me when I was stuck inside of it on a Sunday when where I really wanted to be was in a gym across town, shooting three-pointers. I was crushed. When I'd left the gym the day before, the kids had all been talking about how I was the favorite to win this contest, and all I could do was sit in my room and study and think about how to lift my grades. And I didn't think there was any way to contact Al McClain or anyone at the tournament to let them know I wasn't coming, so I was just a no-show. It was a real low moment, and then I got to school that Monday and heard all about the kid who won the contest, a kid who'd finished in second place in the first round—way behind me. He earned himself a big old trophy, must have been about five feet tall.

I'd wanted that big old trophy for myself, but my father wanted something more for me, something bigger, and this was probably the toughest adjustment of all. To find a way to balance what seemed to be important to my new American friends against what was important to my parents—what was *really* important.

School was my priority, but sports were my passion.

Soon my brothers and I were playing ball on all these different teams, all over the city. School ball, club ball, AAU ball—it was wild. Somehow my parents found a way to make it to most of our games. Sometimes they'd have to split up, just to keep up with our schedules, but they were our biggest fans. All through high school, I used to hear my mother's voice above the noise of the crowd, telling me what to do the same way she used to tell me what to do on our dirt court back home in Lagos.

She'd say, "Shoot the ball, Alski!" She'd say, "Go to the basket, Alski!"

(Yeah, she called me Alski, too. The name really took.)

My brother Johnson was emerging as the best athlete among the four of us. He was a lights-out player—whatever he wanted to happen on the court, he could will it so. When we first got to Boston, he was the only kid in middle school who could dunk, so that was something, but his overall game was just dominant; everything seemed to flow through him. Anthony was the pure shooter of the bunch. He was like our Scottie Pippen. He could kill you outside, but he could also grab a rebound with one hand or dunk on the tallest kid on your team. He could style and he could muscle. And Joseph, who was by now the shortest of us, had turned himself into an outstanding ball handler with tremendous vision. He ran the floor like a general, so he was the point guard in our family.

Mine was a mixture of all of their games, all wrapped up in one. I learned to play with more finesse than I was used to back home. I learned to play smart—to *think* what I wanted to happen before I tried to make it happen. I learned to use the backboard to bail myself out of tough spots.

I was style and muscle, head and heart, inside and outside. I was good to go.

After a while, I started playing for an AAU team called BAAC—the Boston Amateur Athletic Club. Al McClain hooked me up. The club was run by a guy named Leo Papile, who eventually became the director of player personnel for the Celtics. This was like his give-back program to the community, but he really loved working with the local kids. All through high school, that's where I played. Of course, I played for my high school team, too— at "the Burke," Jeremiah E. Burke High School in Dorchester. It wasn't much of a school in terms of academics back then. For a couple of years in there, it had lost its accreditation—I guess because student grades and test scores weren't up to state standards. But my older brothers had gone there, and my younger sister and brother would go there as well, so it was like our family tradition. On the plus side, it had a good basketball program, run by a coach named Abner Logan, though we didn't have a lot of guys go on to play college ball, because few players had the grades to get into a Division I school. We had some of the best players in the state, but they weren't the best students, so this was usually the end of the road for their basketball careers.

Up and down the halls of the Burke, there were kids in and out of trouble. This was a problem in terms of academics, but not really in terms of basketball. The guys on the team tended to be aggressive, hard-charging types; they played the game with the same restless energy they seemed to bring to the classroom, only out on the court it was more of a positive. I would have liked to have been in an environment where I could push myself in the classroom, but the competition was good. The familiarity was good. For a while I thought about going to a prep school, where I might have found a better mind–body balance, but I stayed put.

A big reason for this was football. You see, I wasn't *just* a basketball player by the time I got to high school. In fact, I don't think you can even say that I was mostly or even primarily a basketball player. There was a time, definitely, when basketball was front and center, but football was right up there, too. I was good at football, too. I don't mean to blow smoke my own way, but some people said I was one of the top players in the state. I played quarterback, mostly, and as high school wore on, I started getting recruitment letters from a number of big-time football programs. Every week, there'd be another few letters from coaches, asking me to check out their school, to consider their program. I'd hear from basketball coaches, too, only they tended to be from mid-major type schools: good academic programs, a notch below some of the real basketball powerhouses.

I couldn't pick one sport over the other. My thing was to play both for as long as possible, and that was another good reason to stay put at the Burke. The coaches there knew me and my family. They knew what I could do. They were willing to work with each other and leave me alone to do my thing. Of course, I wasn't the first two-sport athlete to play for my high school, just as I wouldn't be the first two-sport athlete to play in college. (Hey, in the history of the NCAA, there have even been three-sport athletes every here and there.) It's just that, for the most part, two-sport athletes don't usually play in back-to-back seasons. You'll see a lot of football–baseball combinations, because that's a fall and spring deal. The seasons don't really overlap. You'll see football–lacrosse athletes—like the great Jim Brown, one of the greats of both sports. But football–basketball is a tough mix because it's fall and winter, which means you'll have one season starting up while the other is winding down, so it takes a little bit of accommodating.

I made an impact on the football field right away my freshman year. I had a great season, was actually on pace to set a new record for touchdown passes, when I stumbled right into another, even more powerful example of the weight my parents placed on academics over sports. I was fourteen years old, about to break the single-season record, when I was done in by my report card once again. It was a Friday afternoon, just before our last game of the season. I had one more shot at the record that Saturday; I needed one more touchdown pass to tie the record and two to beat it. Even more important, our team had one more shot at the playoffs, so it was a big, big game for me and my teammates—a win-or-go-home-type deal. It also happened to be the day when our first-quarter report cards were handed out, which was always a big, big day in our house.

I tore open my report card on my way to football practice, saw that I got all As, maybe one A minus, and then stuffed the paper into my locker and promptly forgot about it. I forgot to bring it home, too, and that night at dinner, when my brothers and sister were all sharing their report cards with my parents, my father turned to me and said, "Where's your report card, Alex?"

I said, "Oh, I left it at school." I said it like it was no big deal—because really, it was no big deal.

He couldn't believe it. He said, "I need to see your report card, Alex."

I said, "I know. I left it at school. I'm sorry. I'll bring it home Monday."

I assured him that my grades were good and that I only forgot to bring it home because I was racing to practice.

My father was pissed. He didn't say anything, but I could tell he was pissed—only it wasn't until the next morning, when I woke up to get ready to head out to the game, that I knew *how* pissed. Usually, I'd leave my football equipment downstairs by the front door so I could grab it on my way out, but it wasn't there. I looked all over the house, couldn't think where I'd left it. Finally, I saw my helmet and pads chained to the bottom of the basement steps.

Chained!

I fumbled with the lock, tried to break through the chain, and as I did, my father approached, as if from nowhere.

He said, "You won't be playing today, Alex." He said it just like that—plain, matter-of-fact, like he was reading a verdict.

I couldn't believe it, couldn't understand it. I mean, I knew school was important. I knew my grades were important. I knew it was important for me to keep my parents informed about my progress at school. But I'd done well that quarter. I wasn't trying to pull one over on my parents or to keep the truth from them. In fact, I'm sure they knew my grades were good, because I was a good student, a diligent student. I didn't think the punishment fit the crime, and I tried to say as much.

I said, "Daddy, please . . . "

But he cut me off. He said, "I'm sorry, Alex, but you need to bring your report cards home."

This time there was someone I could call. This time I got on the phone to my coach, John Rice. Coach Rice was another fixture on the Boston sports scene. He'd actually been a standout basketball player at UMass Boston, was selected by the Celtics in the ninth round of the 1983 NBA draft, but he also played football and wound up coaching at the Burke. He was the perfect football coach for me because he was cut the same way: He understood my commitment to basketball and football; he knew how hard it could be to play both sports.

I told him the story. I said, "I'm so sorry, Coach, but my father won't let me play."

He said, "Come on, Ski! What type of bullshit is that? You're my QB."

(Yeah, even my high school football coach called me Alski.)

I said, "The school's closed. Maybe you can get someone to open the place up, so I can get to my locker."

For whatever reason, Coach Rice couldn't get me into the school—and even if he'd been able to, I don't know that my father would have unlocked my gear and let me play. I was stuck, grounded. And the thing of it is, I never knew why my father went to the trouble to chain up my gear like that. He could have just told me I couldn't play in the game and that would have been that, but he had a kind of dramatic streak. He liked it when his message came with a little theater.

At the last minute, I appealed to my mother, to see if she could possibly run interference for me on this. She'd been out of the house all morning, and when she came back, I thought there still might be time for me to make it to the game. I raced to get out the story. I said, "Mommy, Daddy chained my gear to the basement steps. He's not letting me play. I forgot to bring home my report card, and now he's not letting me play."

She said, "Why didn't you bring it home?"

I said, "I don't know. I just forgot."

She said, "What were your grades?"

I told her, and even though she already knew the answer and seemed to consider my situation for a moment, she finally said, "Well, Alex, we need to see your report card. You should have brought it home. Next time you'll remember."

We lost the game. We didn't make it to the playoffs. I lost my shot at the record—for that year, anyway. (I came back and broke it my junior year.)

But I never again forgot to bring home my report card, so I guess the message took.

Meanwhile, my teachers were starting to know me as a serious student, and when you teach at a place not known for its serious students, this kind of thing stands out. It stood out to the point where some filmmakers even got in touch with the school to discuss a documentary they wanted to make about an inner-city high school for WGBH-TV, the local PBS station. Somehow the talk turned to me. Among documentary filmmakers, apparently, *inner city youth* was the accepted euphemism for *black urban youth*, but I didn't mind the label. What I did mind, though, was the filmmakers' basic premise, that my part of the story was only interesting because I was succeeding in a classroom setting that didn't place a whole lot of value on academics. That wasn't me. And I didn't think it was a fair depiction of the Burke, either. I'd just completed my freshman year, and already I could see that this wasn't what my high school experience would be about, so my first inclination was to tell these filmmakers I didn't want to participate in their documentary. But then I talked it over with my parents, and we came up with another idea. We thought a more compelling, more truthful story would be to look at how the focus placed on a recruited athlete could somehow inspire other students to extend their reach. It put a whole different spin on it, and the movie people seemed to like the idea, so they started following me around with a camera crew.

The documentary was called *A Day in the Life*. It came out in 2001, during my sophomore year. In my segment, it talked about how I was this fifteen-year-old kid, six-four, a top football player, a top basketball player. And it talked about how I wasn't all that interested in going off to a school like Oklahoma or Texas, how instead I wanted to go to a school like Harvard or Brown—if those schools would have me. And do you know what? The image of our high school began to change, just on the back of this little documentary. Anyway, that's what people started telling me. The Burke went from being known around Boston as this place where kids couldn't get out of their own way, where kids barely graduated, to a place that lifted kids up and out of their circumstances. It was a huge positive for the school and led to a grant from the state for renovation of the building and the expansion of some programs.

But the really great thing about that documentary was that it shined a positive light on our entire community. Wasn't just my segment so much as it was the whole documentary. It set it up so other kids were inspired to excel in the classroom the same way they pushed themselves on the court, on the field. It had a real ripple effect, so I guess you can say it changed the culture at our school—at least a little bit. It made it so it was okay to study hard, to do your homework, to strive. It made it so we weren't content to just go through the motions and put in a minimum amount of effort, just to get by. And it wasn't all on me, this change—not at all. But I was proud to have had a small hand in turning things around.

And it helped me, too. After the documentary came out, it pushed me into this role of being a serious student, so I doubled down on my focus and extra effort and really made my schoolwork a priority. It had always been important, but now it was especially so, and I pushed myself the whole rest of the way. I ended up having a great high school football career *and* a great high school basketball career. People kept telling me that if I committed to a top football program and if I stayed healthy, I could almost count on being a first-round NFL draft pick. But schools with big-time football programs wouldn't have wanted me to play basketball, so that was out. And then, on the other side of the argument, there were a number of smaller, academically oriented schools sending me recruiting letters as well, and people kept telling me that if I committed to one of those schools and things didn't work out for me in professional sports, I could almost count on having a successful career or getting accepted into a great graduate program. It's like I couldn't lose either way. For a while, it looked like I'd be headed to Brown; the school was only forty-five minutes away, in Providence, Rhode Island, and their coaches came to a lot of my games. Harvard was just down the street, and their coaches came, too. But the Ivy League–type schools wanted me to play one sport or the other, not both.

I didn't really have anyone advising me on this. My parents knew what it meant for me to go to college—they knew which schools could open doors for me in the future—but they didn't really know anything about intercollegiate sports. Coaches like John Rice and Al McClain, Abner Logan and Leo Papile, they couldn't really advise me, either. They knew which schools offered the best football opportunities, which schools offered the best basketball opportunities, but they'd never had a player go down this road before. They'd never had a player who wanted to go to the best possible school and to continue to play ball at the highest possible level—on the court *and* on the gridiron.

They'd never had a player who wanted it all.

THURSDAY, FEBRUARY 17, 2011—9:29 A.M. EET

I am sitting on the floor of Mutassim Qaddafi's apartment, trying not to cry.

I am terrified.

I am angry.

I am lost in a hazy jumble of thoughts, wondering how the hell I'll get out of here, how I'll get home, what will happen next.

With my right hand, I continue to press the redial button on my cell phone. Over and over, still. I am calling everyone I know, hoping against hope that a call will go through. Without even thinking about it, I call my friend and teammate, Moustapha Niang, the only other foreign-born player on the Al-Nasr team. He is from Senegal. He is resourceful. He has been here in Libya longer than I have. He knows Benghazi, probably better than I ever will. Probably a part of me is thinking, Moustapha can guide me out of here.

I fall into a kind of rhythm dialing all these phone numbers. Sometimes I do not even wait for the call to go through. My fingers dance across the touch screen as if from memory.

I am shaken from my wondering, from my dialing, by a new set of noises rising from the square to my seventh-floor window. Sirens. Screams. Gunshots. The sounds of war, *I think. I also think this:* Even the sounds of war can become background noise. *It can be so loud one moment, so terrifying, and in the next moment you can hardly hear it. You can go from a killing thunder to a dull hum in nothing flat. And yet the noise is the same. The only change is you get used to it. You find a way to tune it all out and lose yourself in the stupid rhythm of dialing your cell phone, and somewhere in there you lose all sense of where you are and what you're doing.*

I set the phone down on the floor. It is of no use to me, I decide. I crawl to the window to see if the picture outside has changed since I retreated back inside the apartment. I do not have a clear view, but I can make out some kids from the neighborhood. Before there had been mostly men—young men—crowding these streets. Now that the machine-gun massacre has passed, now that the gunfire has slowed, now that the killing has quieted the crowd, a couple dozen children have appeared on the scene. I recognize them from the safety of my apartment. They are the small boys who always gather by our practice fields, playing soccer. When I'd go out for a run, I'd stop to kick the ball around with them. When I'd walk home from the arena, they'd meet me outside to ask for an autograph or a picture. Or they'd wander into the gym to watch us practice, like I was the Pied Piper. These same kids were always following me around the small patch of Benghazi between my apartment and the arena and the Al-Nasr practice complex. And now here they are, these same kids, eight and ten and twelve years old, wielding knives and guns and rifles. It is the strangest, most unsettling picture, seeing them—here, now, like this.

Here, now, like this . . . it makes no sense. I cannot understand what I am seeing. I close my eyes to it, and then quickly open them again, half believing the picture will change. But there they are again, these same kids, running, yelling, holding machetes high in the air, bandannas wrapped around their heads like they are playing at being mercenaries.

It is like a video game to them, I imagine. It cannot be real.

I do not have a next move. Always, on the basketball court, I try to think three or four steps ahead. I know that if I move this way, the defender will react that way, and that I will then counter in a way that causes yet another reaction. There is a whole chain. But here, there is no way to link one action to the next. Everything is random, uncertain.

I can only stare out my window and try to make sense of the senselessness on the street below. That is what it is, how it appears to me. It makes no sense. I cannot begin to take sides, because I cannot begin to understand the issues on one side or the other.

Soon I am drawn to the movements of a small girl. My eyes find her as I search the scene. She looks to be about eight or nine. She wears a plain dress, a hijab to cover her head. She is visibly upset, crying. She runs towards a man I can only assume is her father. Has been her father. He is laying in the dirt, his limbs splayed in every direction, like a chalk outline from a police crime scene. His hair is matted with blood. He is not moving. Surely he is dead.

The girl tries to pull this man who must have been her father by the ankles. She is determined to remove him from the street. She cannot save him, but she can save his dignity. This is how I process what she's doing, how it makes sense, but the girl cannot move the body. It is too much, too heavy. She struggles for a while in this way, and then she is joined by an older woman, whom I take to be her mother. The woman is dressed in a similarly plain dress. Her head is covered in the same manner as the girl's. Together, they continue to struggle. Together, they start to drag the body from the street towards the nearest building. They move slowly, leaving a trail of the man's blood in the dirt as they progress.

It is an agonizing thing to watch, but I cannot look away—an agonizing thing to consider, but I can focus on nothing else.

After a while, just short of the building, the girl and the woman stop with their dragging. They are exhausted from their effort, from their crying. They fall to the dirt and sit behind their body. Their crying becomes wailing. They are unable to move.

THREE | GEORGETOWN

WANTING IT ALL took me only so far.

My dream all along was to go to an Ivy League school. That was the carrot I chased growing up, the ideal. My father taught at Harvard, so that was what I knew, but I would have been just as happy at Yale or Brown. I would have been happy at Dartmouth. I could have seen myself going to any one of those great schools. I wanted to be a doctor—that was my thing, and part of that thing was doing my undergraduate work at the best school possible, in the most challenging environment.

In the end, though, those schools didn't want me unless I would commit to either basketball *or* football; those coaches didn't want me playing both sports. Oh, they wanted me, some of them, but only on their terms. Not mine.

My parents probably thought I was crazy to pass up an Ivy League education for a couple more seasons on the court or on the football field. My brothers certainly thought I was crazy to pass up a shot at a top football program. They kept telling me I had a chance to be a first-round NFL draft choice if I stayed healthy, if I played well . . .

If *this*, if *that* . . .

I took it in like a whole lot of noise. If you want to know the truth, I wasn't thinking about being a professional athlete. If you'd asked me at the time, I might have said I wanted to play in the NFL, but only in the way little kids say they want to grow up to be a football player. It was a leftover fantasy. Same with the idea of playing in the NBA. It wasn't real, wasn't within my control, so on a practical level, I was only thinking about medical school—college first, and then medical school. Playing ball was just something to do to fill the time along the way—and, as long as I was at it, I wanted to keep playing games that mattered, at a high level, while at the same time focusing on my academics in a classroom setting that also mattered, also at a high level.

Most definitely I wanted it all, and it looked like the closest I could get to having it all was at Georgetown University. No, it wasn't Harvard or Yale, but it was a strong academic institution with a big-time basketball program that competed in one of the country's elite athletic conferences, the Big East. Academically, it was probably one of the top basketball schools in the country, along with Duke and Stanford, maybe Vanderbilt, but it also had a lot of juice in my neighborhood. Growing up on Rindge Avenue in Cambridge, just a couple of blocks from where Patrick Ewing lived after his family emigrated from Jamaica, we heard a lot about Georgetown basketball, so that was a big part of the school's appeal. Going there gave me a lot of cred among the local ballers. Ewing had gone there. Allen Iverson had gone there, and at the time he was one of the best players on the planet. They didn't have much of a football program, though. For football, the Georgetown Hoyas competed in the Patriot League, and even though there were some big-time games on their schedule—Miami, Boston College, Army, Navy—they were hardly the most competitive team in the conference, so the pluses and minuses kind of canceled each other out.

For a while, my AAU teammates wanted to stay together and sign as a package. That was the talk all through high school. We would be like our own version of Michigan's Fab Five, we told ourselves, told anyone who'd listen. We had it all figured out. We'd go to Boston College as a unit and be like local all-stars—hometown kids staying put and still making good on a big stage. That would have been a great story, but it's not how it went down. One by one, my buddies splintered off. My best friend signed to play at Michigan. Another signed to play at Iowa State. The others found spots in other programs where there was a good fit. That left me and my Ivy League dreams, which were fizzling for all those other reasons.

Folks at my high school made a big deal out of signing day. It wasn't often that we had a two-sport athlete moving on to a major university, so there was a whole press conference set up. There were news cameras and reporters, and underneath this strange new spotlight, I was already starting to think I wasn't making the best decision. It's like I was making it by default, you know—like I was headed to Georgetown for a bunch of misguided reasons. If it was *just* about academics, I would have gone to an Ivy League school. If it was *just* about football, I would have gone to Texas or Oklahoma. If it was *just* about basketball, I would have gone to a school like Kansas or UCLA. In my head, that's how it would have gone. Georgetown just kind of fit itself into an uncertain middle, and on each level, it felt a little bit like I was settling. I wasn't even there yet, and I was feeling like I was settling. If I was being honest with myself, I would have seen that I was having fourth and fifth thoughts before I could even register any second or third thoughts.

And you have to realize, the Georgetown situation was a football-only type deal. I'd be going on a football scholarship, with only a chance at earning a spot on the basketball team. I'd be a "preferred walk-on"—meaning the basketball coach, Craig Esherick, would give me a good long look once football season was over. If I showed him I could play and earned a spot on the team, he'd work it out with the football coach, Bob Benson, and they'd set it up so I could play both sports.

Wasn't any kind of guarantee—even I could see that—but I was a cocky kid, confident enough in my basketball ability to think I'd have no trouble getting Coach Esherick's attention.

My father knew me pretty well. He could sense something was bothering me. He took me aside after the ceremony and said, "What's with you, Alex? Everything okay?"

Whatever was dogging me, I shrugged it off. I said, "Yeah, I'm okay. Just nerves."

But I wasn't okay. It wasn't just nerves. This was the biggest decision I'd ever had to make, and the ink was barely dry on my making it, and here I was thinking I'd leaned the wrong way. I'd been so determined to prove everyone wrong, to look back at all the coaches and admissions people who'd been telling me I could only play one sport or the other and show them that I could do things my way. That was always a big thing for me, to do things *my way*. Probably it's that kind of single-minded, bullheaded thinking that helped me to be successful on the basketball court, that left me thinking I could exert my will on a game and somehow make a difference, but it tended to muddy things up away from the gym. Here I worried right out of the gate that I'd been so stubbornly focused on having it all, doing it all, that I might be costing myself a shot at really and truly having it all in any one area.

Anyway, I headed off to Georgetown and hoped it would all work out.

Football season came first, of course. I got along well enough with my Georgetown coach, Bob Benson, only I didn't get a chance to play quarterback. Not at first, not at all. This was about the last thing I was expecting, and, once my situation became clear, it should have been the first red flag that I might have picked the wrong school. Or gotten myself into an impossible situation—one I should have seen coming, if I'd known enough to look for it. It turned out Coach Benson didn't even see me as a quarterback—not now, not in the future. In his mind, I was more of an all-around athlete, a player, and his focus in training camp was to find me a position, a place to play. Here I'd had it my head that I could start at QB for a big-time football program, and I couldn't even crack the Hoya backfield. It was a lesson in politics, I guess. And humility. All through the recruiting process, nobody ever promised me a starting job, just the chance to compete for one. But once I got to training camp, it felt to me like Coach Benson already had his mind made up about me. Plus, there was an upperclassman ahead of me on the team's depth chart who came from a real Georgetown legacy family—his parents were big contributors—and there was just no way I was chasing him from the starting lineup. I could have been Joe Montana and I wouldn't have seen the field. This is not a knock on the other quarterback, either. It's not even a knock on Coach Benson, who was in a tough spot himself.

It's just how it was, and I had no choice but to make the best of it—a mantra that would become like the theme to my college career.

The Georgetown coaches turned me into a wide receiver, and I was a good enough athlete that I did okay there. I moved pretty well, had good hands, so even though I wasn't all that comfortable in my new role, I was still able to make some plays. They also had me playing safety, and here again I was quick enough on my feet that I did a credible job, but it wasn't what I'd signed on for. In my head, I hadn't passed up all those other opportunities just to be a backup quarterback and a barely adequate position player on a nothing-special team in a low-major conference. Just setting my situation down on paper, now, in plain, no-bullshit language, puts me back in the mind-set I carried through that first season. And despite being the team's third-string quarterback, I never got to take any snaps from under center during games. Not even in blow-outs. I didn't play a single down at quarterback my entire fresh-man year, so you can bet I was pretty dejected by the time that first season was over. I wouldn't go so far as to say I was pissed, but I was disappointed, I'll say that. Way, way disappointed. Mostly, I resented all that time spent at practice, all that time in the training room, all that time away from the classroom, travel-ing to games.

And, soon enough, all that time away from basketball.

Eventually, that first football season bumped right into my first basketball season. That's what happens when the seasons overlap like that, only here I think it cost me in the first-impressions department. Coach Esherick was in his own tough spot. He'd succeeded John Thompson a couple of years earlier, and Thompson was a Georgetown legend, so there were a lot of eyes on Esherick when he took over the program. He'd been Thompson's assistant for almost twenty years, but he couldn't make a move without being compared to his former boss. His teams did okay—they made it all the way to the Sweet Sixteen in the 2001 NCAA tournament—but overall they played .500 basketball, or just about, so there was a lot of pressure on him to get the most out of his players, to make his own mark. Coach Benson was good to his word. He'd set it up so I could try out for Coach Esherick as a kind of preferred walk-on, but it didn't help that I had to miss most of Coach Esherick's preseason. On some days, I had to double up: I'd hit the football field first and then head to the court, and after a hard practice with Coach Benson, I'd be dragging. I wasn't able to play at my best, and, as a result, I had no shot at making Coach Esherick's team.

I don't mean to sound all sour grapes or come off like I was entitled to any type of special treatment, because that's not the way I'm cut, and it's totally not what my frustration was about, but I want to make sure I accurately present my state of mind at that time in my life. I want to stress that the only reason I'd gone to Georgetown was because I thought it was my only chance to play two sports at this kind of high level. I took that promise of a preferred walk-on opportunity as a done deal, because I was extremely confident about my game. It never even occurred to me that I wouldn't make the team, so that's what I signed on for. The academics were great and the campus was beautiful, and these factors had also played into my decision to go to Georgetown. I'd be in an exciting city, meeting all kinds of interesting, dedicated people, but that would have been the case at any of the other top, top schools I was considering. Now that I was at Georgetown, though, I was a little thrown by what was happening on the field, on the court. Like I said, I wanted it all, and this wasn't what I was expecting, wasn't even close. And that misfire on the basketball front just extended the disappointment of that first football season. It didn't help that the basketball team struggled through a tough, tough season. They ended up with the worst overall record of any Georgetown team in thirty years—pretty much since the start of the John Thompson era. In my heart, I knew I could have helped the team and found a way to contribute, to maybe turn some of those losses into wins, but it wasn't meant to be. The way it worked out, there were six other freshmen on that team, and they'd all worked hard to make an impression back in preseason, to make up for the loss of All-American Mike Sweetney to the NBA draft, but I couldn't always be there to make my own case, so I went home that summer thinking I'd messed up. Thinking I'd had all these other options in terms of playing college ball and in terms of the school itself and that I'd somehow made the worst possible choice. Thinking I hadn't been able to take good and full advantage of the opportunities Georgetown might have presented to me—and that I might never have the chance to do just that.

I didn't say anything, though. Remember, my whole bullheaded thing was to prove everyone wrong, to do it my way—and now that it was starting to look like my way might not be working out, I kept it to myself. I didn't want to hear any kind of *I told you so!* comments from my parents, from my brothers, from my coaches back home. I'm sure they all knew my freshman year hadn't really worked out, but I wasn't about to let on. Whenever anyone asked, I'd just talk about how it was an adjustment, how I was still finding my way, that type of thing.

Folks back home knew me as an athlete. My family knew me as an athlete and a student. And the people at Georgetown . . . well, I'm not sure they knew what to make of me. I struggled, man—let's just say that. My whole life, I'd seen sports as an outlet, a way to help me get a good education, a place to channel my energies while I was getting that good education, so I spent some time balancing all those different parts of my identity.

That whole summer, I tried my best to stay fit and focused. I went back to school early, tried to get myself in shape, tried to get a jump start on some summer classes, maybe get out in front of my coursework a little bit, ahead of the football season. The whole time, I tried to think about what went wrong that first year and what I could do to set those things right as a sophomore, and by the end of the summer, I had a positive attitude—or at least I thought I had a positive attitude. I even thought I might find a way to push my way onto the basketball team, if everything broke right for me. But after a couple of weeks of intense practices and scrimmages with the football team, I could see that my sophomore year would be more of the same. I could see that the same legacy quarterback was slotted in as the starter. I could see that I wouldn't have time for any of the premed classes I'd have to take. Also, Coach Esherick had been fired as the basketball coach right after my freshman season, following a loss to Boston College in the first round of the Big East tournament, and with a new coach coming in (John Thompson III), I knew he'd want to bring some of his own players into the mix, so my long-shot dreams of latching on to the basketball team were becoming less and less likely.

So what did I do? Well, to say that I decided to make a change suggests that I gave it a whole lot of active, careful thought, when in reality it was kind of an impulsive move. It was like the decision was made for me, and I could only follow along. And so I came back to my room after football practice one afternoon and just started packing up my stuff. Fall classes were due to start later that week, and I was hit with this wave of unhappiness. I could close my eyes and see the rest of the year unfolding in front of me, and it was like I was looking at a whole blank wall of nothing. I couldn't see anything good, anything positive coming out of either side of my situation, the football side or the basketball side. I caught myself thinking this was supposed to be a joyful, worry-free time in my life, but I was just miserable and not liking my chances of being able to turn things around, so before I could even think things through, I threw all my gear together and made hasty plans to head back home.

I called my brother Joseph to tell him what was up. He was, like, my go-to guy for making big, life-altering decisions, but he couldn't talk me down from this one. All he could do, really, was get me to take a deep breath, to maybe sleep on it, see how things looked in the morning, but I already knew how things would look in the morning. They'd look pretty much the same.

The one thing Joseph and I could agree on was that it would be a mistake to tell our parents. In fact, I kept it from them until I landed at Logan Airport in Boston the next day. Once I was in Boston, at least, it felt to me like I'd crossed some point of no return and my folks couldn't send me back to Georgetown, so I called from the airport to let them know I was on my way home. It caught them completely by surprise, to where there was nothing to say. They were in shock, I think, and, frankly, so was I. Numb. Two days later, my boxes arrived from school with all my worldly possessions, and I was overcome by a huge feeling of relief. It's like those boxes represented this great weight, and the great weight had been lifted—and the weird thing is, I hadn't fully realized that I'd been carrying that weight all along.

—⚅—

My parents still talk about that day I came home from Georgetown unannounced—my father especially. They were completely thrown by it, couldn't understand it, thought I'd made the kind of hasty decision that would ruin my life. Who knows, maybe they were right. Maybe all the shit that's happened since spun out from that one decision. Maybe I'd had all these great opportunities laying in wait, and I'd just tossed them aside on an impulse. Maybe I'd been afraid to push myself, to be great in any one area, and so I let myself hang back on this nothing-special middle ground and wait for something good to happen. Maybe I was just young and bullheaded and felt the coaches at Georgetown weren't treating me right. But then I look back and think, *Hey, it wasn't working out. That's all.*

Honestly, I didn't think I could have ever been happy at Georgetown. I didn't see my situation getting any better. All that tension and uncertainty was even spilling into the classroom, starting to affect my studies in a negative way, and I didn't know how to keep that from happening. It was nothing against the school itself or any of the terrific people I met there, but I just didn't fit. I didn't fit on the field, on the court, anywhere. Medical school, that didn't quite fit either, so I came home knowing I'd have to shake things up. Knowing I couldn't stay in my parents' house without some kind of plan.

Knowing . . . *what*, exactly? Knowing shit, I guess.

He never said it, but I knew my father was disappointed. In me. In the situation. In this new reality. He was an athlete—this was true enough—but sports had never been the kind of big deal to him that they were to me and my brothers. Remember, this was a guy who could have probably made the Nigerian national team if he'd wanted to pull himself away from work, but that had never been what sports were about for him. They were an outlet, that's all. They weren't an end, they were a means to an end. In this way, I was a lot different than my father, I guess. To him, my education was the real end game, and he worried that I might have jeopardized my chances of getting into medical school. Pulling out of Georgetown like that, at the last minute, would raise a lot of questions, not just in coaches but also in admissions officers, so I started answering them in all these haphazard ways. To me, the education piece was important, but it was just a piece. I wanted the whole package. I wanted to shine on the field and on the court.

I was home for just a few days, trying to figure out my next move, not wanting the coming school year to get away from me, when a buddy of mine mentioned that he was playing ball at a community college up in Warwick, Rhode Island. It was about forty-five minutes from my house, so it was close enough to home to make going there no big deal. First, though, I checked it out online. There was a pretty New England campus, great facilities—even some kick-ass hotel suites for the athletes. And from what I could tell, they played a decent brand of basketball. It was Division II, but my thinking was that I could make some noise at that level and maybe play my way back to a Division I program before too long.

Mostly, it struck me as a place where I could retrench, regroup. A place to focus on my studies and maybe earn back whatever reputation I might have had as a basketball player. A place to try and make the best of it all over again.

I could have gone a whole other route, I suppose. I could have looked at a long list of Division III schools in our area, New England Small College Athletic Conference (NESCAC) schools like Amherst and Tufts, Williams and Wesleyan, where I would have gotten an outstanding education, where the basketball coaches would have been happy to have me, but I knew the odds of rising from one of those programs to a top Division I program were pretty damn long. And besides, those Division III schools didn't give athletic scholarships. There were academic scholarships and certain educational grants available to eligible student athletes, but I couldn't count on that to cover the full cost of a private undergraduate education. True, the academics would have been great, just like at Georgetown. I would have been surrounded by bright students in a stimulating intellectual environment, but in addition to being a little out of reach financially, I didn't think these schools would help me on the basketball front. I'd never get back on the recruiting radar. Don't get me wrong, they played some good ball at those schools, and every once in a while they'd produce a player to watch, but for the most part, it was considered a lower level of basketball. I could have poured in twenty points a night and nobody would have noticed.

Division II was the way to go, I told myself—and, for now, the Community College of Rhode Island (CCRI) seemed like my best bet. I had my buddy reach out to the coach, Dave Chevalier, to see if there might be room for me in his plans. I realized it was late for this type of recruiting. I knew the guy's roster was probably set, but I had nothing else going on. I was out of ideas. I kind of figured I was done with medical school, even though I still had an interest in health and science. Also, I kind of figured I was done with football, because I'd seen how difficult it was to keep both of those balls in the air. More and more, I was thinking basketball would be my ticket back to a top academic school. In truth, I hadn't left myself very many options, so my thinking had as much to do with timing as it did with choosing one sport over another or thinking one sport provided me with a better opportunity than the other. I'd bolted Georgetown at the last possible minute, under the worst possible circumstances, which put the calendar against me in terms of re-upping with another foot-ball program. The football season was already under way, but the basketball season was still taking shape. Plus, I reached out to the NCAA clearinghouse office, because I worried that my one year of football might in some way have cost me a freshman year of basket-ball as well. I'd never played my way on to the Georgetown basketball team, but I did practice with them a bunch of times, so I wanted to be sure I still had a full four years of basketball eligibility.

I knew the Ivy League coaches who'd been recruiting me the year before wouldn't touch me after the way I'd left Georgetown, not just yet. But it turned out the CCRI basketball program was decent enough, and they had supernice facilities, so on the same whim that led me to pack up and leave Georgetown, I drove up in my buddy's truck to check the place out.

Coach Chevalier knew I was coming. My buddy Halim Lopes called ahead to tell him about me, which meant that now the coach had been checking me out, too. He knew I'd had all these Division I coaches chasing me the year before. He knew I'd kind of flamed out at Georgetown. He couldn't imagine the chain of events that might have brought me to his office in the CCRI athletic complex, so as soon as we shook hands, he put it to me plain.

He said, "What the fuck are you doing here?"

So I told him what the fuck I was doing there, and this seemed to satisfy his curiosity and answer any concerns he might have had about my sudden departure from Georgetown.

He said, "You got your transcript?"

I handed it over. Coach Chevalier gave it a quick glance and that was that. I ended up having a great year there, became the school's first-ever junior college All-American, and off of that one bounce-back season, I let myself think I'd be back in the mix before long.

It didn't quite work out that way, though. It turned out Division I basketball coaches have long memories. I was still a wild card in their minds. Taking me on meant taking a risk—even I could see that—so it would take a little more than a single season of Division II ball to get them to think about reaching back out to me. Division I football coaches, though, had a somewhat shorter memory, because I started getting a bunch of calls from programs that had recruited me the first time around. I don't know why that was, but it just was. Maybe it's because they had so many more slots to fill on their teams, so many more scholarships to throw around.

One call that stands out now, looking back, was from Mike McQueary, an assistant coach at Penn State, who was already fairly well known in college football circles but who has since come to national attention as one of the key figures in the child-sex-abuse scandal that almost shut down that program. At the time, McQueary was just looking to shore up his QB depth chart, and my name must have popped up on one of his lists.

He said, "I hear you're not at Georgetown anymore. How'd you like to enroll here?"

The Penn State call wasn't the only one I received, and I mention it here only to show how my athletic career could have still gone in an entirely different direction, where I could have competed with Anthony Morelli and Michael Robinson for the Nittany Lions' starting quarterback spot, even at this eleventh hour. But by this point, I'd wrapped my head around basketball in such a way that I could think of nothing else. My father was a little disappointed about this, I think, because he'd become a great football fan since he'd moved to the States. He just loved the game, loved watching me play, thought I had something special. But I'd set football aside, along with the idea of medical school. My new and improved plan was built around basketball: win a spot on a good college team, maybe play my way into the NBA, and pocket a good education along the way as a kind of fallback. But it was still a little too soon for some of the bigger and better programs to take an interest. I was still a bit of a loose screw for their tastes, so for a while it was looking like I'd just re-up at CCRI for my sophomore season.

But then something happened that set me off. We'd had a great year, earned a spot in the Division II NCAA postseason tournament, which was just tremendous. Coach Chevalier had put together a good group of solid players and set it up so we could really play to our strengths. One of our strengths was defense, but then Coach went and left our best defender back in Rhode Island when we traveled to Illinois for the tournament. I couldn't understand it—still don't, to be honest. This kid had pulled some bonehead move—he'd forgotten his ID, I think—and rather than wait for him to double-back and get it, Coach decided to just leave him behind. It was like his own spin on that life lesson my father used to throw at me over my grades, my report card, only here it struck me as a little off point. Here it meant a punishment for the whole team. It kept us from achieving something we'd worked towards all season, all on the back of a mostly meaningless mistake that was hardly a big deal. It didn't seem like the right time to go teaching this kid a life lesson, you know.

My teammates and I all knew we were screwed without this player. We made our case to the coach, but he wouldn't listen. He heard us out and said, "We don't need him."

But we did need him, it turned out. Without him, we had no defensive presence. Without him, we had no depth. We had a short rotation as it was already, maybe six or seven guys getting into the game in any kind of meaningful way, and now that we were playing these win-or-go-home tournament games, Coach ended up playing the same five guys all the time. Somehow we got by the first couple of games just on grit and hustle. By the third or fourth game, though, we were gassed. We had a deep run, hung around until late in the tournament, but we had nothing left, and I left Illinois thinking it was bullshit that the rest of our team had been penalized in this way.

I thought, *Okay, this one kid might have screwed up a little, but the rest of us, we were the ones who ended up paying for it,* so I was done with Coach Chevalier and CCRI at that point. In my head, I was done.

—⟁—

Up next was another stop on my Making the Best of It, Getting My Shit Back Together Community College Tour—this time up at Monroe Community College, in Rochester, New York. This time I threw in with a terrific coach named Jerry Burns. Coach Burns was good friends with the Van Gundy brothers—he'd played for Stan Van Gundy at Castleton State College—and I came away thinking there must be something in the water in Upstate New York because these guys could all coach. They knew the game.

We actually played Monroe when I was at CCRI, so I knew they were well coached. I knew they had a bunch of guys who could really play and that most of them were coming back. One of them was a good friend of mine, actually, a guy I'd played against in high school, and he kept talking up the school, talking up Rochester. He told me they played a bunch of Division I teams, told me Coach Burns ran a strong program, so I drove up to see for myself. Oh, man, that place was beautiful. It looked like a full-on university. Pretty campus. Great facilities. Nice dorms. Nothing like you'd expect a community college to look. And Rochester was cool, man. It was a decent-size city with a whole lot going on, so once it became clear to me there'd be no scholarship offers from any of the Division I schools that once had me in their sights, I started to think this was a good place for me to continue my climb.

Jerry Burns couldn't have been more welcoming. He was happy to have me, but he was tough on me. He wasn't about to let me slide. On the first day of preseason, I guess he thought I was slacking. I guess I came in thinking I was *all that*, thinking I was some hot shit junior college All-American. He was probably right to call me out on this. I probably had a little too much swagger to my game.

Whatever I was putting out, Coach Burns wasn't about to take my shit. He treated me like I was some green freshman, like I'd never played college basketball before. He wouldn't let anything slide. And then, after practice, he found a reason to follow me into the locker room, stood right at the sink next to me while I was washing my hands. He didn't do this in any kind of menacing way, like he was chasing me down to chew me out or anything. No, sir. He just played it kind of casual. Turned on the faucet in front of him and pretended to wash his own hands, until our eyes met in the mirror. And then he just hit me with it. He said, "You've got to practice harder."

Just like that. *You've got to practice harder.* Looking at me in the mirror the whole time. He didn't say it like he was mad or disappointed. He just said it flat, like he was making a simple observation, and it took, man. It took. From that day on, every practice, I busted my ass. Still, to this day, I bust my ass.

You've got to practice harder.

They were like marching orders. So I marched.

It was a good season, both for me individually and for our team. We turned a lot of heads. And, soon enough, Coach Burns started hearing from Division I coaches who wanted to know if I was some kind of head case. That's how it goes in the recruiting game. They reach out to your coach first to get his take. The year before, in Rhode Island, everybody thought there must have been something terribly wrong with my makeup, to go from being this standout high school player to not even making the team at Georgetown to community college. They'd see me play, read their reports, talk to my coaches, and wonder what the hell was going on with me. Basically, they looked away. There were enough level-headed ball players out there without these giant question marks hanging over them that the big-time coaches had no reason to take me seriously.

But Jerry Burns took me seriously, and he saw to it that the Division I coaches who started calling him took me seriously, too. They'd call Coach Burns and ask, "This Owumi kid, what's his story?" Or "What's up with Alex? Is he the same player he was back in high school?"

And each time out, Coach Burns would talk me up. He'd say, "Yeah, man. He's tremendous. He shouldn't be playing here."

I was grateful for his support, for the not-so-gentle push Coach Burns gave me in that locker room mirror, for the opportunity he gave me to take back a college basketball career that might have gotten away from me. Mostly, I was just happy to be playing good ball. It felt to me like I was moving in the right direction.

Classes were kind of an afterthought at Monroe—for me, anyway. I'd been challenged by some of my courses at Georgetown, but they didn't expect a whole lot out of us at these community colleges. I had some good teachers, some interesting courses, but the workload wasn't much. Most of my friends didn't place a high priority on their academics, which in turn made it easy for me to go at it the same way. I mean, as long as I was getting good grades,

I saw no reason to bust my ass in the classroom. I figured I'd save that for the basketball court.

San Diego State, UCLA, Rutgers . . . all these Division I schools came calling. To this day, I've got no idea how serious they were about me, but they came calling. Only by this time I'd found a new obstacle to throw in my path. It wasn't so much an obstacle as it was a *condition* I set—and yet as a recruiting bust at Georgetown with just two years of junior college ball on my résumé, I was in no position to set conditions. I was trying to be a good guy, I guess, trying to help out a friend from home. His name was Anthony Searcy, and at six-eight and maybe 240 pounds, he was a potentially dominating presence on the basketball court. Trouble was, he was stuck playing ball for FIT—a Division III program in New York City. This alone didn't strike me as such a terrible thing when Anthony first filled me in on his plans, because I'd never heard of FIT. It's only when I learned that the initials stood for Fashion Institute of Technology that I realized the box Anthony was in. Lots of folks, they've got no idea FIT even has a men's basketball team, and I had no idea how the hell Anthony wound up playing there, but he couldn't get a look from a Division I coach. Nobody respected the program enough to even watch one of Anthony's games, even with his size. You'd think a kid built like that, with even an ounce or two of talent, could find his way into a decent college basketball program, but that's not how it was shaking out for him.

He called me up one day just to bullshit, just to see if I'd made any kind of decision on where I was going next. He said, "You sign yet, Ski?"

I said, "Not yet, man. Thinking about San Diego State. Thinking about Cal. Far from home, but hey."

He said, "Shit, man. I can't even get an offer. These schools, I'm calling them. They're not calling me. And they don't want to hear from me anyway. They don't respect this program."

We got to talking, and as we did, I started thinking that I could help Anthony out. He hadn't asked for any help, and I hadn't offered, but once I put the phone down, I started thinking it was the right thing to do. I started thinking I was in a good spot, in a position to maybe call my own shots. You see, Anthony wasn't just another friend from home. Our connection ran a little deeper than that. He'd been my running buddy growing up in Boston. We were like cousins—in fact, we used to tell people we were related in a distant, once-or-twice-removed kind of way—but I wasn't helping him out because of blood. I was helping him out because I could, that's all. Not because it was an obligation, but because it was a privilege. Because he needed a hand to pull him up and out of a bad spot. The way things were shaking out for him, he couldn't afford to stay at FIT, which as a Division III school didn't hand out any scholarships. He needed to get his degree, to change the direction of his life, and I thought I could help make that happen for him, so I started talking Anthony up every time I'd hear from a new coach. I got it in my head that I could maybe present the two of us as a kind of package deal—an inside game *and* an outside game, to really turn around a program. It was probably a stupid, selfless move—but I never said I wasn't stupid, and I kind of like it that I'm selfless, so there you go.

Once again, I didn't have anyone advising me on this. I had my parents, my brothers, my coaches back home. I had Coach Burns, who wanted to see my game take me as far as it could, but I was running my own show. Following my gut, improvising. This was probably a mistake, looking back. And I should have seen it was a mistake at the time. One by one, these big-time coaches started falling away. I was already a bit of a wild card after the way I'd left Georgetown and bounced around playing community college ball. Coaches, scouts, recruiters who'd seen me play said I had a lot of talent—I got high marks from them on the floor—but my career to that point hadn't exactly been a slam dunk. It's like I could only make good decisions on the basketball court—away from the gym, I was a mess. Nobody knew what to make of me, and here I was announcing that I would only play for a coach who would also make room for my friend from back home. I wasn't doing it to be a prima donna or to pump out my chest. I was doing it because I'd decided Anthony Searcy could use my help and that I was in a good position to offer it.

So that was that. And for a while there, it looked like I'd have to try to walk on at some school or other, until I got a call one day from Jason Cable, an assistant coach at Alcorn State University. He was a young guy, just a couple of years older than me, trying to hustle his way into the coaching game.

He said, "Hey, man. I know it's a long shot, but would you consider coming here for a visit?"

I'd never heard of Alcorn State before Jason called, but he filled me in. He told me Alcorn State was a small black college in rural Mississippi, told me they played in the Southwestern Athletic Conference, which he said was a strong mid-major conference. Just as important, they were coming off a good season, with most of their players returning.

As soon as Jason finished making his pitch, I started making mine. Told him all about my buddy Anthony. I said, "You know what? I got a player for you. Six-eight, two-forty, hell of a rebounder, hell of an athlete. Good kid."

I can't say for sure, but I'm guessing Jason Cable wasn't expecting me to turn the tables on him like this. I think I caught him by surprise. For one thing, he was surprised I didn't politely hang up on him and that I stayed on the phone with him for so long, which he took as a sign of interest. But the bigger surprise, probably, was to have a recruit take the opportunity to press another player on him. And I didn't just press—it was a full-court press. I said, "Look, man, this kid needs a break. He can play for you. He can help you. And if you sign him, I promise you, I'll sign with you too. Just give him a look, that's all I'm asking."

Jason wasn't authorized to act on my push—I probably should have figured as much—but he did say he'd check with the head coach, Samuel West, and get back to me. He did say he'd check up on Anthony. And he did. The first call he made was to my AAU coach, Leo Papile, but Anthony had never played for him. Coach Papile knew who Anthony was, of course. He'd seen him play here and there, he knew we hung around together, but he couldn't talk about Anthony's makeup or his work ethic or any of the stuff coaches want to know about when they're recruiting. He could talk about me, though. He said, "Anthony Searcy never played for me. Alex did. I can vouch for Alex. And I can guarantee that if Alex vouches for Anthony, you'll have a guy who'll fit right in. You'll win a lot of games."

To this day, I don't know why I pushed so hard for Anthony, why I attached him to my basketball future, but he'd had it tough, man. No, it wasn't about blood, but there was a feeling of family. We went back a long way. He grew up in a not-so-great part of Boston, in Section 8 project housing. He was raised by his grandmother, and it was looking more and more like he'd have to go back to Boston to help her out. He needed a break. He needed a scholarship, a clear path to a college degree, and it felt to me like a blessing to try and help him get one.

And sure enough, Jason Cable got with Coach West and discussed their options. As far as I know, they never even looked at a single piece of film on Anthony, but they went on my say-so, and on Leo Papile's take on my say-so, and offered Anthony a scholarship. They actually sent him the paperwork before reaching back out to me, and Anthony was just through-the-roof excited. I hadn't really told him what I was up to, other than to tell him I'd try to talk him up when I could, so the call kind of came out of the blue for him. He called me as soon as Alcorn State got in touch. He said, "I can't believe you did this for me, man. I don't know what to say."

I said, "Just say we're going to Alcorn State."

I didn't even make a visit to check the place out—probably because I didn't want to give myself a reason to bail on my decision. That whole spring and summer leading up to the 2006–07 season, I just tried to focus on my game and staying in shape. But the thing of it is, I kept getting calls from some of these other top schools, wondering if I'd signed, trying to fill their last-minute roster spots. I remember getting a call, late, from UCLA, telling me they still had a spot for me, and I got off the phone thinking, *What the hell am I doing?*

But I'd given my word to Jason Cable and Samuel West. I'd given my word to Anthony Searcy. I was headed to Mississippi.

I am thinking only of escape. I am running through a dozen different scenarios, imagining myself away from this building, from this city, from this hell. I am unable to think what will happen next. I have nothing to go on. I cannot see a way out.

I rise and cross to the kitchen sink. I want to splash some water on my face. I'm thinking maybe it will help me think more clearly, but I can't get the faucet to work. Just a few moments ago, before everything turned to shit, the water was working just fine. I was able to wash and brush my teeth and get ready for practice, but now the tap is dry. It makes a sick, hollow, empty sound, like it's sucking up air. I turn the handles this way and that but get back nothing, so I try the bathroom sink. Again, nothing. Like an idiot, I hang back for a beat, almost like I'm hiding, waiting to pounce, and then I try the faucet again, thinking maybe I'll surprise it into working. Then I hit the thing with the heel of my palm. Then I reach under the sink and hit the pipes a couple of times. Then I go back to the kitchen sink and repeat the same stupid motions.

I am frustrated on top of confused on top of frustrated. Also, I am quickly distracted by the sound of crying. All along, I have heard the screams and shouts and cries of the protesters drifting through the closed windows of my apartment, but this new set of noises is not a collection of cries. It is a single, tiny, aching cry. It is like a baby fussing, right here in my kitchen. It sounds like nothing up against all those other, darker noises, but at the same time it sounds like everything because it is closer to home. Because it is real, something I can know. Because it is upon me. It takes a couple of wails before I figure out that the crying is coming from the baby next door, in my landlord's apartment. Our kitchens are connected by a small window, almost like a pass-through, so I open the shutters on my side and call out to the baby's big sister. Her name is Miriam. She is about eleven years old. She is the only one in her family who speaks English—in fact, her English is perfect. We have had many nice visits talking about basketball and school and Libya. Her family, through Miriam, has been good to me.

I'm yelling, "Miriam! Miriam!"

In response, I only hear more crying, so I yell to her again. Finally, Miriam comes to her side of the window. She looks like she's been crying, too, only her tears have now passed. She is too young to have to deal with something like this, but that seems to be exactly what she's doing: dealing. She must be frantic and scared, same as me, but she comes to the window to talk to me like we are just wishing each other a good morning.

She says, "Alex." That's all, just my name.

I say, "Miriam, I can hear your little sister. I can hear her crying. Is she hurt?"

"No," Miriam says. "She is just hungry. There's nothing for her to eat."

It is just a coincidence, I believe, that my neighbors have no food, but that is how many people live here in Benghazi. It is not like in the States, where we fill our shelves and lay in our supplies. Back home, we shop for the week. Here the people shop for what they are about to eat. Everything is fresh. In general, this is what I've noticed. Libyans go to the market to buy what they need to prepare their next meal, and it appears no one has been able to leave my neighbors' apartment to shop for breakfast.

I have been in Benghazi for only six weeks, but I have become the same way. Recently, I have been shopping for what I am about to eat, for what I might eat the next day. But I also keep a little bit of food, some staples, which I immediately offer to Miriam and her family. A couple of gallons of water, some bread, some meat, some cheese. Not a lot, but it would have been enough to hold me for another few days. Still, I am not thinking I will be holed up in this apartment for another few days. I am not thinking I will be hungry anytime soon, so I give Miriam what I have. I only keep a few slices of bread for myself, two eggs, and a little bit of milk for later.

And there is also this: As I open my fridge to collect the meat and cheese, I realize our power is out. I reach for the light switch on the kitchen wall and confirm that it is dead. I cannot think what this might mean. No water. No power. Whatever this means, it cannot be good.

There is nothing to do with this new piece of information except to notice it. Power or no power, I am still trapped, scared. Power or no power, protesters are being gunned down in the street like zombies in a video game. Power or no power, the baby next door is still hungry, so I collect this small bunch of food for my neighbors and walk with it to the cutout in my kitchen wall. The bundle is too big to pass through our kitchen pass-through—the opening is too high for Miriam to reach—so I motion for her to meet me in the hallway. I smile to show her it will be okay, and when she meets me, I am struck by how little she is. How she is just a child, dealing with whatever is going on in the street outside our building.

"I do not have much," I say, handing over the food. "Please tell your parents. Please tell them I wish I had more to share."

Miriam thanks me for the food and retreats into her apartment, and I retreat into mine. As soon as I do, I reach again for my phone.

Once again, I dial and dial. Once again, there is the same "call failed" message on my screen.

Next I open my laptop, thinking maybe I can get Internet service. The computer has been in the charger overnight, so there should be a full battery. The power will not be a problem. But there is no server. Yes, the battery is charged, but it does me no good.

I start to realize I am cut off completely from the outside world. I already know this on some level, but it takes trying everything again and again to know it fully. I am completely off the grid. No water. No power. No phone. No Internet. I am like that tree in a forest, the one they used to make us think about back in high school. If I fall, there will be no one to hear me. No one will know. My only connection to life beyond the apartment of Mutassim Qaddafi is the windows that can only keep the chaos of the street to a dull hum. And yet I am drawn to the windows once more. There is a new kind of shouting coming from the other side. A new commotion. I peer through the glass and see that what I am hearing are the sounds of revolution. For the moment, the police have backed away from the scene. Where there was once a standoff, there is now madness and confusion. There is an angry, swelling mob. There is smoke coming from the police station. I do not have a full, clear view of the building, but I can see that it is on fire. I can see that it is under attack. I can see a group of men pulling the bodies of police officers from the smoke. I can see children running from the scene with handguns, machetes, rifles.

I close my eyes and imagine the change in scenery from just a few days before. Yes, following the news in Egypt of Mubarak's resignation, the crowd in the main square of Benghazi had grown bigger, more restless. Yes, there had been tension in the air, but not enough for me to notice, not really. It is only now, looking back, that I can see the change. When it was happening, I chose to look away. I let myself believe this was the way of this part of the world. I had set it up in my head that the only thing I should focus on was our upcoming game against Al-Ahly Benghazi, and as I stand here now, trying to understand the disorder outside my window, I cannot stop wondering when it was that basketball stopped mattering most of all, when it will matter again.

FOUR | ANTIBES

THE FIRST WEEK OF AUGUST 2006, Anthony and I flew from T. F. Green Airport in Providence, Rhode Island, to Jackson, Mississippi. The whole way there, we were pumping each other up. We set it out like a serious adventure, like we were going back in time, headed to one of the country's historically black colleges. No, Alcorn State had never been a true basketball powerhouse, but they'd sent a few players to the NBA over the years; they'd knocked off some top teams, earned a couple berths to the NIT and NCAA tournaments. (On the football front, they'd sent a long list of players to the NFL, including Steve McNair and Donald Driver.) At the very least, we thought, we'd be going up against some of the best players in the country, so it was a chance to grow our games, see what we had on more of a national stage.

It wasn't the easiest drive from the airport to Lorman, Mississippi. It's way, way out in the country. To say it's in the middle of nowhere makes it sound like nowhere is even on the map. We got a ride out of Jackson, the state capital, and it seemed like a nice enough place, a decent city, and I thought if we were just outside of Jackson, we'd be okay—there'd be stuff to do, things to see—but we kept driving and driving. Forty-five minutes later, we got to Vicksburg, which struck us as another nice place, so we still thought we'd be okay, but it turned out we still had a long way to go. I don't think I'd ever been on such a long stretch of nothing. We drove for another forty, fifty minutes until we reached a dirt road. All we could see was farmland—just a bunch of cows and chickens and falling-down buildings. It was another seven miles from that dirt road to an even smaller dirt road, then another two or three miles to the worst road yet. Finally, we pulled into what looked like a dirt driveway with a sign that said it was the main entrance to the school—home of the Alcorn State Braves, our new team.

All along this driveway, left and right, all we could see were trailers—you know, like those portable double-wides you see on construction sites. No buildings. No grand old campus architecture. Nothing like that. Just a ramshackle, sorry-ass place. It looked nothing like the school's Web site, nothing like we'd been picturing. The place was pretty empty—most students wouldn't be arriving for another day or two—but Samuel West and Jason Cable came out to meet us. They couldn't have been nicer, more welcoming. They had a couple of players with them, too, so it was like they rolled out the welcome mat for us—the Alcorn State version, at least.

Coach West turned out to be a great, great guy. Nothing like any basketball coach I've ever played for, before then or since. For some reason, his players called him Weezy-Wee. Don't know why, but that's what we called him, and he didn't seem to mind the name at all. He wore it like a big old smile. Weezy-Wee was focused on God and church and school and basketball, in that order. Anthony and I hadn't realized we were signing on for such a spiritual journey, but this was just as well with us. We'd both come from churchgoing households. We'd each read the Bible and worshipped in our own way. But Alcorn State wasn't known as a religious school, so we were a little thrown at first. We hadn't expected so much team prayer and devotions—sometimes Coach had us sitting still and praying and devoting for a full forty-five minutes before or after practice—so it really stamped our time with him, really forced us to look inward and upward.

This, I came to think, was a good, good thing.

We got a quick tour of the campus and ended up at our dormitory. The plan was for me and Anthony to room together in a double, only we got to our room and saw we already had another roommate—a giant rat running across the floor. I saw that and thought, *Oh, man, what are we into here?* Coach looked at us kind of funny, half hoping we hadn't seen what he'd clearly just seen, but the giant rat wasn't even the worst of it. The room was dark and dirty, almost like a dungeon. It smelled kind of funny, too. But Weezy-Wee was such a cheerful guy, he pretended like it was a room at the Copley Plaza Hotel. He said, "This is where you'll be staying, boys. Make yourselves at home."

I said, "You can't be serious?"

Coach wanted to be helpful, wanted us to be comfortable, so he said, "Let's see what else we got." That's the great thing about a small school, we were learning: They can go out of their way to be accommodating. Only here there wasn't much in the way of accommodations. He took us to what he called the apartments, which of course sounded a whole lot nicer, but which in fact were those double-wide trailers we'd passed on the way in. They were completely bare, with no furniture at all, and isolated from the main part of the campus, so we went back to the dormitory. That giant rat was looking pretty good by comparison.

Another thing we learned soon enough was that black colleges in the South hadn't quite figured out the coed living thing. The dorms were all single sex, and the women's dorm was all the way on the other side of campus, which we all thought really, really sucked. Plus, our room was on the sixth floor, with no elevator, which also really, really sucked. There was an elevator in the dorm, but it hadn't worked in years, and there was no money in the school's budget to fix it, so we spent a lot of time on the staircase. Coach tried to put a positive spin on the situation by telling us it was a good way to work on our cardio, the same way he tried to put a positive spin on every negative in our path.

The gym was nice enough, but there was only bleacher-type seating, and the locker room and training facilities were mostly old-school and underequipped. But what the place lacked in modern amenities it made up for in history. The first things we noticed when we walked into the Health, Physical Education, and Recreation Athletic Complex were the purple and gold banners and the plaques honoring Davey Whitney, Alcorn State's legendary coach, who was known around campus as the Wiz. He was a former Negro League baseball player who somehow ended up coaching basketball at Alcorn State for decades. His teams won twelve SWAC titles and more than six hundred games, so it really felt like we were stepping into this basketball cathedral. It wasn't exactly Pauley Pavilion at UCLA, but the place reeked of history. Okay, so it was a run-down, bare-bones cathedral, and mostly it

just reeked, but it was filled with all this great tradition, it had
hosted so many big games, and I remember sitting with Anthony
after one of our first practices and talking about how we could
maybe help lift the program back to what it once was. That was
like our charge to each other, our commitment to give something
back to a program that was giving us such a great opportunity.

It didn't quite work out that way, I'm afraid. There were a lot
of factors working against us. The athletic department had next
to no money. We couldn't put our names on the backs of our
uniforms, because we had to give them back at the end of the
season so next year's team could use them. We drove to away
games in crappy buses, squeezed into seats that were designed
for middle school kids. We ate greasy food and slept in cheap
motels. We were tired and sore and bent out of shape from those
trips, which almost always ended in some kind of disappointment or other.

Most noticeable, most meaningful of all, though, was that we
only had a three-man coaching staff—Samuel West, Jason Cable,
and a graduate assistant named Sean Hill. There was no athletic
trainer, no nutritionist, no real support staff—no good way to
recruit or develop players. But Weezy-Wee, I had to give him
credit, man. He kept us playing with a joyful outlook. He gathered us for prayers, for devotions, and helped us learn to appreciate what it was we did have. He was always so up, so enthusiastic,
even when the game wasn't going our way. And he tried to layer
in all these teachable moments whenever we traveled. Like in our
first year, on a trip to Alabama State during Black History Month,
he had us stop at a civil rights museum. We'd also have to take
turns standing in the aisle of the bus as we were rolling along

these back roads and recite a short report on a prominent African American. At first I thought it was kind of corny to have to do stuff like this, but I started looking forward to those presentations. Some schools have stupid hazing rituals—they make you sing some fight song or memorize some rap lyric—but the Alcorn State Braves put a different twist on that kind of thing. This Black History Month presentation thing was a good example. Some guys chose Jesse Jackson, Malcolm X, the playwright Langston Hughes, and on and on. Me, I chose my grandfather, who'd helped to integrate that PGA course in Dorchester, Massachusetts, where I grew up, and Coach pulled me aside afterwards and told me how much he appreciated the way I'd shared a little bit of my family history with the assignment.

He seemed really moved by it, and I was moved that he'd been moved.

Coach West was a great storyteller, and he'd hold forth on those long bus rides like we were sitting around a campfire. Sometimes the whole team would be listening in. Sometimes it'd be just the two of you, huddled in the same seat. He had this one story he used to tell into the ground that seemed to always end with the same kicker. He'd say, "If you put me one hundred miles in the desert, I will come back to you with a bucket of chicken and a milkshake."

He'd say it like it was the moral of the story, but none of us could ever figure out what the hell he was talking about.

On the basketball court, we struggled that first year. We drew the University of Texas in our season opener, which was a ridiculous mismatch. Remember, this was back in 2006, Kevin Durant's freshman year, so I had to go out and guard a guy who even then was probably one of the best basketball players in the country, and I didn't do such a good job of it. Kevin had six or seven inches on me, and he could play. Oh, he could play. Anthony had to guard Dexter Pittman, a big seven-footer who now plays for the Memphis Grizzlies, and Dexter just destroyed my boy down low. Anthony was a little out of his league, I'm afraid. I was overmatched in this game, too, and only managed to hit one of seven shots from the floor in just sixteen minutes. Even though we jumped out to a surprising 9–1 lead in the opening minutes, Texas roared back, closing the half on a 47–9 run. I don't think I'd ever been on the wrong end of such a lopsided final score—103–44—so it was a real Welcome to College Basketball–type moment for me, but I was able to adjust after a while. I found my rhythm as the season wore on, found my way.

Anthony, though . . . he had a hard time keeping up. For all his size and strength, it was a tough go for him. Weezy-Wee was such a positive guy, he never got on me for insisting he offer Anthony a scholarship as part of my deal, even though Anthony wasn't able to make the kind of contribution we were all expecting out of him. And it's not like Anthony was any kind of weak link on our team. He had size, he had skills, but he just couldn't put it together against big-time competition. He wasn't any kind of game changer. Even Anthony would say as much. But Coach knew we'd given this kid a tremendous opportunity, and Anthony was an outstanding teammate. Weezy-Wee was genuinely pleased to have him around. He really practiced what he preached, I guess you could say.

We ended up 11–19 that first year, my junior season, but we got better as the year went along. We went into the off-season thinking we could maybe turn things around, only we drew another ridiculous opponent at the start of our 2007–08 season. This time we went up against Oklahoma and Blake Griffin in our second game of the season, and Griffin just ate up my pal Anthony. Just destroyed him, man. Ended up scoring only 16 points, but once Oklahoma got up big, he didn't play all that much the rest of the way. Nothing against Anthony, but Griffin was a force of nature that night, grabbing rebounds with one hand, driving the lane and spinning and throwing down one of his tomahawk dunks. You could see, even then, that Griffin was going to be a special player. Already he was a special player—and we could not keep him from his game.

By the way, I didn't have such a great game against Oklahoma, either. Actually, I stunk the place up, going just 2–14 from the field.

Academically, Anthony did all right. He took full advantage of the opportunity, and this of course was the most important thing. He stayed on his books, got his degree, set himself up to become a high school teacher back in Boston.

We played a killer schedule that year. Ten of our first twelve games were on the road. From Oklahoma to Hawaii, Montana to New Mexico and on to Nebraska, we traveled all over. It was grueling. It didn't help that our seven-foot big man tore his ACL during our Midnight Madness scrimmage to start the season, so we were up against it right out of the gate. We opened with a 1–12 record, and that one win came against an NAIA school, Southern–New Orleans, which was like a Division II school. It was brutal, and it didn't get much better after that, even though we did manage to play .500 ball within our conference.

The silver lining was that it was a decent season for me personally. I averaged close to 15 points per game and was named team MVP. It would have been nice to win a bunch more games and post a more competitive record, but I was happy with how I'd played. Happy with my game.

And, amazingly, I was happy with my short time at Alcorn State. Thrilled, actually. I never would have guessed it going in, with the rats and the run-down, isolated campus, but I became a real proud alum. I just loved, loved, loved that school, everything about it. I ended up majoring in broadcast journalism, which might serve me well somewhere down the road when I'm done playing, but even more than that, I made great, great friends and had some outstanding professors. Most of all, I got to spend two years under the influence of Samuel West, one of the most remarkable coaches I've ever had a chance to know—a guy who got me thinking I could do anything on a basketball court, anything away from a basketball court, as long as I put my heart into it.

What's amazing, too, is that I finished college convinced that my best basketball was ahead of me. That hadn't been my plan going in. Coming out of high school, I'd only thought to play ball to kind of underline my time in the classroom, to reach for the mind–body balance I thought you were supposed to aspire to in college. Remember, I started out thinking I would go on to medical school. That was always the goal. But something changed. Somewhere on my way from Georgetown to the Community College of Rhode Island, from Monroe Community College in Rochester, New York, to Alcorn State University in Lorman, Mississippi, some light went on that left me thinking my basketball journey wasn't done just yet.

—Ⱳ—

Here's the harsh lesson of life after college basketball: You are where you played.

At least that's how it seemed to me after my second and final season at Alcorn State. Fact is, I'd played in the middle of nowhere on a nothing-special team in a nothing-special conference. I don't mean to hate on my school or the SWAC, but it was almost like playing in a vacuum in terms of getting any kind of national attention. If you saw me play that year, it was probably only against one of those top, top teams we faced early on, when we were getting thumped. Still, a part of me thought I might be selected in the 2008 NBA draft that spring. It wasn't because I was arrogant or because I had an inflated sense of my abilities as a basketball player, I don't think. No, it was because I could play, bottom line. But it was also because of my old AAU coach, Leo Papile, who still had a lot of ties to the Boston Celtics organization—all around the league, in fact. He was talking me up and talking me up, trying to get me on every team's board.

Even I could see that I wasn't about to get chosen early on in the draft, though. I would go late or not at all. It was a crowded draft class, with a lot of talented players coming out of school. Derrick Rose, O. J. Mayo, Russell Westbrook . . . It was a guard-heavy year, but I really thought I had a shot. Were there ten guards bigger, better, or stronger than me in that draft? Maybe. Were there twenty? I didn't think so. And as draft day approached, I started to make more of a name for myself. I actually had some very competitive, very encouraging predraft workouts—one down in Orlando and a few back home with the Celtics. They called me back in a couple times to see what they could see. They liked the numbers I had put up playing for a losing team. They liked that I could rebound, that I could pass. They liked that I played hard on defense. I actually sat through the draft with my mother, thinking it was going to be a special night, but my heart broke a little when the Celtics weighed in with the thirtieth and final pick of the first round. A lot of basketball folks thought the Celtics would go with a guard that year, in that spot, so I was hopeful they might look to me, but that's not how it shook out. They took another guard instead—J. R. Giddens, out of the University of New Mexico.

I have to admit it burned me that the Celtics tapped Giddens, because I thought I was a better player than him. We'd faced each other a bunch of times—not just in college but in AAU ball. I knew his game, and I knew mine, and it felt to me like the Celtics should have looked my way instead, especially because I was a local kid. We matched up pretty well, only I thought I had Giddens beat by every measure. This is not me blowing smoke. This is me telling it straight. What it came down to, I think, was basketball pedigree. His was better than mine, that's all. He played for a bigger program. And he started out at an even bigger program, since he'd been recruited out of high school by Roy Williams at Kansas. He'd been a McDonald's High School All-American, while I was just a nominee. Basically, J. R. Giddens had me beat on paper, while I had him beat on the court—and, in the end, the Celtics went with how it looked on paper.

That's just how it goes, right? And maybe there's a good reason for this. Maybe basketball executives have learned over the years that players from top programs have better upside than players from lesser programs. Maybe there's a little extra something in that player's DNA, a better foundation, whatever.

Now, obviously, I don't know if that's how it shook out. At the time, I just let my mind run wild and this was what I came up with, but even now, with perspective, I have to think the Celtics were my best shot that year. It makes sense. I mean, I was a local kid, which was always a big plus. They'd worked me out three times—three weeks in a row. Each time, they pumped me up with all kinds of positive feedback, told me they were looking at me hard, told me I might be able to fill a need for them, but then they went and picked J. R. Giddens, and with their second-round pick, the sixtieth pick overall, they grabbed a seven-foot center from Turkey, Semih Erden.

The way it works in these predraft workouts is they bring in a bunch of guys, and then they look at you every which way, in all these different situations. There were usually seven or eight other players in my sessions, and they always had me matched up with another guard, another kid who had essentially the same build, the same game. And you do battle. One-on-one, two-on-two, however they set it up. The session itself is run by the assistant coaches, but the top brass is there, too, looking on. These Boston workouts were held in the team's practice facility in Waltham, Massachusetts. Celtics head coach Doc Rivers was there, but he stayed off to the side. He probably watched some of the workouts from his office, but he was paying attention, taking notes. Danny Ainge, the general manager, was right there on the floor. That was kind of cool, kind of great. I remembered him from the tail end of his playing days and thought maybe he'd *get* me because he'd been a two-sport athlete, too, reaching the major leagues with the Toronto Blue Jays. I thought maybe he'd see me as some kind of kindred spirit. Or, more likely, that his own experience would help to explain away some of the gaps in my résumé.

For those who've never been to a predraft workout, I'll say this: The sessions are superintense. They work you hard, man. They measure your vertical leap, your body fat. They stretch you out, warm you up. They take out the stopwatch and time your shuttle runs. It's like they're trying to break you, see how you hold up against all this pressure, but I didn't feel any pressure in that gym. I was just playing my ass off in my official Celtics gear, doing my thing, making a case for myself.

Afterwards, they take you aside and talk to you. They tell you what they liked, what they didn't like. They tell you how things might go if they do wind up taking you with one of their picks. Sometimes, they ask what *you're* looking for—if you can be happy being a role player, coming off the bench, that kind of thing. And they pump you for information a little bit, like asking if you've worked out for any other teams, where some of your friends or teammates have been working out, whatever. Then they send you on your way. They say you'll hear from them if they want to follow up, and I took the fact that they kept calling me back as a good sign. I was hopeful, encouraged.

I was disappointed to come out of that draft empty. Absolutely, I was bumming, but I wasn't flat-out dejected. I wasn't despairing or thinking this was the end of the road for me in terms of the NBA. Hell, no. I mean, there's only two rounds, only room for sixty players, and about two-thirds of them were underclassmen coming out early or international players who'd still need another couple years of seasoning before they were NBA ready. By my math, that meant there were just twenty or so players from my year who got the nod, twenty or so of my peers, and I could live with that. I wasn't happy about it, that wasn't the way I would have written it, but I could accept it. The rest of us were free agents, man. That was the positive spin. We could sign with any team instead of just the one team that drafted us, so that was the glass-half-full way to look at it.

The morning after the draft, I still popped out of bed thinking I would someday play in the NBA, and as far as I could tell, there were now a couple of ways to make that happen. The obvious move was to play in the D-League—the NBA developmental league, which was like the game's official minor league organization in the States. A lot of guys who get overlooked in the draft sign with the D-League and keep playing, maybe catch the eye of an NBA scout, maybe get a ten-day contract. Some of the guys who do get claimed in the draft get assigned by their team to a D-League franchise to polish up their games, because the big club feels they're not quite ready to contribute at the NBA level.

The one knock on the D-League, though, is the money. Salaries are structured. There are A slots, B slots, and C slots. A players make the most money—roughly $5,000 per month over the course of the season. If you're a high-level Division I player, undrafted, you're probably going to be assigned to an A slot. An NBA veteran trying to work his way back into the league is probably an A player as well. But if you're a lower-level Division I player or if you're coming out of nowhere, you'll be a B or C player, and you might only make $4,000 or $3,000 per month. So the money goes from halfway decent to nothing much at all, but it's not like you're in any kind of position to negotiate your own salary or designate your slot. It's all handled by the league.

The other move, the more adventurous move, is to play overseas, where the money can be pretty good, where you've got some leverage as a player, if you're willing to trade the exposure you might get playing in front of NBA scouts every night for playing halfway around the world. In exchange, you'll make more money—*way* more money—and in some countries, in some leagues, you'll play before big, loud crowds in giant arenas. You'll move around like some rap star, traveling first class, instead of as some has-been or wannabe, riding the bus.

It's a tough call, which way to go, and in my case it was even tougher because I started getting offers from some high-level European teams for some really good money. It's all about how your game will translate overseas. And in my case, I think it helped that I had some mixed blood, that I was both Nigerian and American. I was a good ball handler. I could pass, shoot, defend. My game lent itself pretty well to a bunch of different styles of play—that's what I was told—and I started getting a lot of calls, so I had to take them seriously. The most interesting offer came from a team in the Pro B French league, AL Roche-la-Molière. They were based in Antibes, a small city in the south of France. The money was good. And the French federation was known to take its basketball very seriously. They'd had a lot of players over the years who went on to play in the NBA, guys like Tony Parker and Mickael Pietrus. And they had fans. Big-time, basketball-crazy fans. The arenas were on the small side compared to the NBA, maybe four or five thousand, but they were packed every night. From what I was hearing, the French were crazy for their basketball, and after playing so long in the Siberia of the SWAC, with just a couple hundred people at most of our games, the idea of playing in front of a big, pulsing crowd was appealing to me. Compared to the D-League, it'd be like night and day. It'd be popping.

So I weighed my options, found myself leaning towards France. Found myself thinking a big stage would be nice. Big money, too—about three times what I would have made with a D-League contract, plus they'd set me up in a nice apartment, cover my meals, my expenses.

It wasn't much of a decision, really. It was kind of a no-brainer. I was young, confident, curious . . . where'd you think I'd wind up?

—⁂—

Antibes is actually a resort-type town on the Mediterranean, so there was a whole lot going on there. I'd looked it up online when the offer came in, and it made Lorman, Mississippi, look like the middle of nowhere all over again, in a bunch of new ways. There was great food, great nightlife. And beautiful, beautiful women—like, world-class beautiful. And the setting? Oh, man, it was just magnificent. Like a picture postcard.

I'd set it up in my head that the place was like Disney World for twentysomething Nigerian Americans with a little bit of money in their pockets, so just on the creature comfort and extracurricular levels, I stepped off the plane thinking I'd made the right decision. And believe me, the place didn't disappoint. The people were great, too. On the basketball level, though, I wasn't so sure. It took a while for me to adjust to the French style of play. Back in the States, I was used to playing an up-tempo game. I was always pushing the action. Everything was fast, turbocharged, in-your-face. I loved to run the floor, full tilt, and then dish off to an open man on the wing or take it hard to the hole myself. But here in France, the pace of play was a little slower, a little more disciplined. Plays took some time developing, and I just wasn't used to that.

Also, it was more of a coach's game in France. I'd played for some great coaches, but we were always given a lot of freedom. We were encouraged to improvise—to take what the game gave us. But the European game was much more structured. It's like they wanted you to follow a script, and I'd never been that kind of player.

From time to time, I'd get so frustrated with this uneasy transition that I thought I'd made a big mistake, playing in France. I got to thinking I'd be further along if I'd signed on with some D-League team. I had this fantasy that I would have been tearing up the league, making a big impression, and that by midseason I would have landed a ten-day contract and found a way to stick with some NBA team or another. I would have been all set, instead of having to slow down my game to fit with the international style of play.

Back home, you play with a group of guys for a couple of weeks, you get to know their tendencies. You read each other, play off each other. But, like I said, the European game is more by the book. Everybody tends to play the same way. There's less of a feel to the game; it's more regimented. And it's slower. Not because the French players are themselves any slower, any less athletic, but because they take their time with the ball. They take their time getting into position, getting set, always careful to make the proper play, the proper move, so it felt to me like I really had to dial down my game. The first couple of weeks, I was making a ton of turnovers, mostly because I was trying to think a few steps ahead of my teammates. I was trying to predict where they'd go next and lead them with a pass, only they weren't expecting it, because they'd never played that way before.

Unfortunately, I was slow to pick up on this. Slow and a bit bigheaded, I'll admit. My first impulse was to try to get my AL Roche teammates to adapt their game to mine, to step it up—but, naturally, that wasn't about to happen. It wasn't because there was a language barrier so much as there was a basketball barrier. It took me a while to realize that, yeah, I might have been the starting point guard, but there were four other guys on the floor and just one of me. It made no sense for me to push everyone else to play my way. The only thing to do, really, was to change my game to match up with theirs, so that's what I did. Eventually. I settled in, toned it down to where we were all finally playing the same game.

After that, the season kind of fell into place. I ended up winning league MVP honors, averaging more than seventeen points and six rebounds per game. I made a lot of great friends, too. Didn't learn a whole lot of French, though. I picked up a couple of words—I could order in a restaurant, get myself around town—but I couldn't come close to holding a conversation. The French fans seemed to know this, because they did a lot of their cheering in English—not just when they were cheering for me, but a lot of their cheering in general. Apparently, the chant of "Defense, defense!" is the same all over the world.

Normally, I'm a team player, a good guy to have around. At least that's my goal. I try to do whatever my coach asks of me in practice, and maybe a little bit more if I can. But here in France, there were a whole lot of distractions, and I'm ashamed to admit it, but I stepped out of line a time or two. One of those times, it got me benched. What happened was, the Cannes Film Festival was going on, and I wanted to check it out, so I decided to bail on a Friday afternoon practice. It was a dumb-ass, selfish move, but I got it in my head that this was something I just had to experience. So I boarded a train to Cannes and walked around all those great big yachts, soaking in the scene. I didn't meet any stars, but I did see George Clooney. I saw the guys from *Entourage*. I saw a ton of beautiful women—like, insanely beautiful women—and for a couple of hours I got to see what all the noise was about.

I figured it would cost me, but only a little. Figured my coach would fine me for missing practice, and that would be that. But it cost me a lot more, because it worked out that the day I ditched practice was the day before a game, and our coach was a hard-liner about that type of thing. I knew all of this, of course, but I was rash, impulsive. I got it in my head to go, and I just went. I had a blast, but as soon as I got back, Coach lit into me pretty good, told me he'd have to sit me out. At first I thought he'd just sit me for a quarter, maybe the first half of our game. But no, he sat me for two whole games, and of course I didn't get paid for those two games. On top of that, I cheated myself out of whatever bonus I might have earned for winning those two games. Worst of all, I lost whatever respect and goodwill I'd built with my team. Coach was pissed, and he had every right to be. There was even talk of sending me home and voiding my contract, but I didn't think that would happen. I thought the team managers were just trying to scare me. But that was just me, still not learning my lesson. I mean, I'd let my teammates down. I'd let my coach down. It was unprofessional. It was stupid. And I knew it was all those things all along, but I went ahead and skipped practice anyway, thinking I'd only get a slap on the wrist. So I deserved whatever fines and reprimands these guys wanted to throw at me. I belonged in their doghouse. Yeah, for an afternoon, I got to see how the other half lived. I got to check out these fine, fine-looking women on the beach, on these pricey-ass yachts. I got to hang with the beautiful people. But it cost me, man. Better believe it, it cost me. And I learned the hard way that there's no such thing as stepping just a little bit out of line.

Either you take the game seriously or you don't.

As a team, we didn't have such a good season. We lost more than we won, but I caught a lot of nice attention. For the first time since high school, I had fans—people who followed my comings and goings on the court, who waited outside the gym after my games for a picture or an autograph, who wrote about me in the newspaper. I wouldn't say it went to my head or anything like that, but I didn't mind it, not at all. The level of competition was probably a notch or two below what it would have been in the D-League back home, but there were all these other advantages to playing in France that convinced me I'd made the right move. We traveled in style, while the guys I used to play with who were banging on the D-League circuit were always complaining about the long bus rides, the shitty food, the nothing-special facilities. The team owners took really good care of us, sent us around the country in a sweet coach bus or on charter flights. They put us up in decent hotels. And the facilities were first-rate. Some of the arenas were on the small side, especially our own, but they were

all tricked out with modern, comfortable locker rooms and training equipment.

All in all, I had to count my season in France as a success,
although I worried I might not have made much of a name for
myself in NBA front offices. They knew me a little bit when I left
for France, but I worried that after a year away they knew me a
little less, so I told myself it'd be smart to find a place to play in
the States for the next while. I told myself I'd saved a little bit of
money, since I'd basically been living expense-free for the past
bunch of months, and the wise thing to do with that money was
to invest it in myself, maybe buy myself another shot back home.

That shot back home found me almost straightaway.

I met a man named Rob Spon, who was a scout for the Cleveland
Cavaliers. He was originally from Pittsburgh, and he was now the
head coach of a team called the Manchester Millrats in the Premier
Basketball League (PBL)—a minor league, Canadian-American
outfit with teams based in Buffalo, Vermont, Rochester, Halifax,
and Quebec.

Manchester, New Hampshire, was about forty-five minutes
from my parents' house in Boston, so I drove up to watch these
guys play. They had some really great players on the roster—guys
I'd known from the Boston area, guys who'd played in the
D-League, guys who'd played in the NBA—and I thought the
level of play was pretty high. If you're comparing it to baseball,
say, this would have been like Double A. The D-League and some
of the better European leagues, they'd be like Triple A, so it felt

to me like a good place to park myself and get back to playing organized ball on home soil.

Also, Coach Spon had a ton of connections—he knew most of the general managers in the NBA, most of the key basketball executives—so I thought of this as a good stepping-stone sort of move. Rob told me his specialty was finding diamond-in-the-rough-type players like Jamario Moon, whom he helped sign to the Toronto Raptors after Jamario had bounced around in the D-League, the United States Basketball League, the Mexican league—even the Harlem Globetrotters. I already knew a little of Jamario's background, because we were cut in a lot of the same ways. Jamario had also played some community college ball, same as me, so I drew a lot of inspiration from his story. Frankly, that's one of the main reasons I was so quick to throw in with Rob in the first place, because I got to thinking that if he could find a diamond-in-the-rough guy like Jamario Moon, playing in all these out-of-the-way places, and set him off on an NBA career, then maybe he could do the same thing for me.

On top of all that, Rob Spon was a good dude. That came across in a big-time way. He seemed to really want to help his players get to the next level, and one of the ways he tried to make that happen was to run an excellent system. So it was a real happy landing for me, to fall in with this group at just that time. I'd had a decent run in France, saved a bunch of money, and now it felt like time to get myself back in the game.

The real difference between the PBL and the D-League was depth. I found this out as soon as I started playing in Manchester. D-League teams had talent up and down the roster—maybe nine or ten guys on each team who could make a strong case for a ten-day NBA contract, maybe even a decent NBA career if they caught a couple of breaks and worked hard. PBL teams were maybe four or five guys deep in that kind of talent, so we could run out a strong starting five, give or take, but after that it was a crapshoot. It meant our practices were a little less intense, only because there weren't enough strong players to go around. So over time I guess it meant that D-League players were better able to grow their games, because they were almost always going up against some serious competition. But when we were firing on all cylinders, man, could we play, and we set off on a nice run to start the season.

The comparison to minor league baseball fits in terms of crowds, too. Folks turned out for these games, so that was a nice kick. We'd roll into town and play a hard-fought game, and we'd be lifted by all that energy in the arena. And there were usually scouts in the stands, too. Even if there weren't any scouts at all for any one particular game, we'd play as if there were. A lot of times, Rob would pull us aside after a game, or sometimes at halftime, and tell us there was some dude from the Toronto Raptors or the Milwaukee Bucks asking about one of us. His thing was, he wouldn't always tell us who the scout had come to see. It's like he wanted us all to feel like we were being scouted, to play like every touch, every possession mattered—not just for the outcome of this one game, but for the outcome of our career.

Sometimes the talk was more specific. Sometimes he'd send one of us off to work out with an NBA club or to practice with some group he'd put together for some kind of scouting combine, so he was always trying to put us out there, to set it up so we could get seen.

We played our way into the league semifinals that one year I was with the Millrats, which we lost to the Rochester Razor-Sharks. That was a pretty intense series. Rochester was the class of the league. They had the biggest budget, the biggest arena, the most hard-core fans. I used to hear about that team when I was going to Monroe Community College up there, basically because they were the only game in town. There was no professional basketball in that region (though Rochester did once support an NBA team), so they filled that arena every night. They sold a ton of merchandise. Whipped the fans into a mini frenzy. And that place was rockin', man. It was crazy.

All in all, it was a good spot for me, playing in the PBL, not too far from home. And who knows, I might have re-upped with Manchester for another season, but after Rochester bounced us from the playoffs, Coach Spon decided to move on, so I figured it was time for me to move on, too.

He'd decided to work full-time as a scout, to devote all his energies to finding another diamond in the rough, so I took this as a charge to make myself into one of his next diamonds. All I had to do was find a way to shine.

Before I could shine on the basketball court, a light went on in my personal life. I met someone—and this wasn't just any someone. This was someone special, someone I could see myself with for the rest of my life. And—get this!—I could see this right away, almost from the moment we got to talking.

The moment we got to talking came on June 14, 2010. I'll never forget the date or the night we met.

Her name was Alexis Jones. She was an actress, model, and singer from New Orleans—she'd appeared in a bunch of movies and television shows and sung all over the world with her sister. My sister-in-law Monique fixed us up. I was visiting my brother in Atlanta, and Monique took me to an event at Justin's, the famous restaurant on Peachtree Street owned by music mogul Sean Combs. We were kind of bored, doing some hard-core people watching, and Monique started asking me about my love life, about the kinds of girls I liked to date. The truth was, I'd been on the road so long, I hadn't had a proper girlfriend in a good long while, and Monique kind of picked up on that. She said she had a friend she wanted me to meet, said she was from Louisiana, from a good family. Said she'd been through a lot.

At some point, Monique pulled out her phone and showed me a picture of her friend, and I was knocked out. No lie, this girl was gorgeous. And it just so happened that Alexis had just moved to Atlanta to try to get something going with her acting career and her singing career with her sister, so after a couple of minutes, Monique said, "Why don't I just text her, see if she's doing anything right now?"

Thirty minutes later, Alexis walked in the door and took my breath away. I hate to use such a tired, old line like that, but it's the God's honest truth. For a moment, I couldn't breathe. Literally and truly. I took one look at this girl and I sat straight up in my chair. I'd been slouching, hanging, but I watched Alexis cross to the bar area where we were sitting, and right away I started thinking about my posture, started thinking I'd do well to make a good first impression. Before we even said two words to each other, she had me thinking I wanted to be a better person.

As first impressions go, Alexis made a killer one. She walked like Naomi Campbell. As soon as she came through the door, all eyes were on her—mine most of all. She just had that type of presence. She had her hair up in a bun, had on a brown tank top and a pair of superskinny blue jeans, and she looked absolutely perfect.

Like I said, for a beat or two, I couldn't breathe.

I can't imagine what kind of first impression I might have made, slouching like that, but it was enough to take me to a second one, at least.

Monique found some reason to disappear and leave us alone, and we fell into the easiest, most natural conversation. It's like I was hanging with someone I'd known my whole life instead of just a few minutes, and Alexis and I spent the whole rest of that night just talking and talking. I got her whole life story—the youngest of three girls, grew up on General Pershing Street in the Third Ward. Her mom was one of the last of the authentic Creole chefs in New Orleans. The Third Ward was one of the parts of uptown New Orleans that was completely destroyed by Hurricane Katrina. Alexis's family lost everything, she told me. The house she grew up in, everything. Her father had been a bit of a local legend, owned a limo service and a reception hall, had played a little bit of professional basketball himself, but his businesses were completely wiped out by Katrina. He lost his entire fleet, and he was so distraught, so distressed, he died of a heart attack about four months later. A couple weeks after that, Alexis lost her grandmother. And then, a couple weeks after *that*, she lost her other grandmother and an uncle, so it was just one devastation on top of another. Her father had been the most important man in Alexis's life. She'd been going to school at Louisiana State University, getting a singing group going with her sister Arin. They called themselves Elysian Fieldz, and they'd just signed a record deal with Universal Records and Derrty Entertainment when Katrina struck and Alexis's world was tossed and turned. She had to leave school and move with her entire family into a hotel room in Baton Rouge—eight people in all, living in one hotel room.

She was still reeling from all of that, was finally getting her life back together. She'd gone back to LSU and earned her degree, and now she was in Atlanta to work on her singing career. As she sat across from me and unloaded all of this *stuff* on me, I kept thinking, *Man, this is one amazing woman. To find a way to keep it together, to keep going, to keep moving forward . . . after all the dominoes in her life just kind of toppled, one by one.*

I told her my story, too. It wasn't nearly as devastating, but I guess it had its own measure of tossing and turning and disappointment, and I think we both felt a powerful connection—right away, that very first night. In fact, as soon as Alexis dropped me off at my apartment, I called my sister-in-law and said, "Thank you, thank you, thank you. This person's incredible."

But I couldn't get the words out fast enough before Monique's phone started ringing with another call—Alexis, calling to say pretty much the same thing about me.

Two days later, Alexis and I hung out. We went to the movies, to dinner, took a walk in the park. The whole time, I felt myself being drawn closer and closer to this woman, and after a couple of hours I finally turned to her and said, "You know what? We should get engaged."

When we tell people this story now, it comes across like I was joking, but I was serious. Maybe not dead serious, but pretty damn serious. I had this crazy idea in my head, and I put it out there. I told Alexis I was tired of being in a relationship where you're just boyfriend and girlfriend and you move along on that path for a while and see how it works out. I told her we should just flip it and start with getting engaged and see how it works out from there.

She said, "My mother would kill us!"

I heard that and thought, *Hey, at least she didn't shoot me down. At least she didn't tell me I was out of my mind.*

I am lost in a mess of crazy thoughts. My mind is all over the place and no place at all. I am sitting on the floor with my back to the wall by the front door, as if I am guarding the place—but, of course, I am helpless against whatever is going on outside. My head is filled with images I want to wish away. The little girl dragging her father's body across the street. The two uniformed officers gunning down the protesters. The children looting the police station and wielding machetes and handguns, like mini terrorists.

It is too much to take in, too much to consider. Just too much.

Suddenly, I am jolted from my crazy thinking by a pounding at my door. It is a big, heavy, steel door, and the pounding comes through like thunder, like a clash of metal against metal. If it is meant to be a knock, I do not have time to answer it, because as I stand and move towards the door, it crashes open. Two soldiers dressed in military greens come barreling through, and from the way they're carrying their weapons, I can only assume that the clash-pounding was from the butts of their AK-47s.

One of the soldiers barks out an order to me in Arabic, but in response I can only throw my hands in the air to show I am unarmed. To show I am not any kind of threat. Also, I make some stupid gesture meant to show that I am an American basketball player, which probably includes pointing to the warm-up gear I'm wearing and pretending to dribble.

Apparently, I make some sort of ridiculous sense to the other soldier, because he says, "ID. ID."

I hold up a finger like I'm asking for a minute and reach into my gear bag for my passport and my player card—a laminated piece of

identification I've been required to carry with me at all times that lists
my name, the team I play for, my age, my nationality.

 The two soldiers look at my player card suspiciously, and then
back at me—also suspiciously. They mumble to each other in Arabic
and seem to agree that I am no threat, that I belong here in this apart-
ment, that they should probably let me alone. And so they do. They
back out of the apartment, looking just as menacing on the way out
as they'd looked on the way in. I push the heavy door closed behind
them, hard, leaning into it an exaggerated way, as if by forcibly
shutting out the world I can keep myself safe and whole. I can pretend
I haven't seen the things I have just seen.

 I lean against the door and slide back down to the floor. To think.
To not think at all. I do not know what to do. I do not have a next
move. I can only sit and wait and think and not think. I can only close
my eyes and imagine that I am home, safe, or that I am down at the
practice facility playing ball or that the world as I know it is still
somehow the same.

 These soldiers, I don't even know if they're good guys or bad guys.
I don't know which side of this fight they are on, which side my coach,
my teammates, my driver are on . . . which side I should be on. These
armed soldiers have left me alone, for now, but I don't know why. Is
it because they are on the side of Qaddafi, and I am clearly here as a
guest of his family? Is it because they are on the side of the protesters,
and they are afraid to touch me because I am an American? My head
fills with a new mess of crazy thoughts, and none of them make sense.
Nothing is clear. There is only confusion, fear, paranoia. There is only
the slow, sick realization that I might never make it home, that what-
ever crap is going down outside this door is going to get worse before it
gets better.

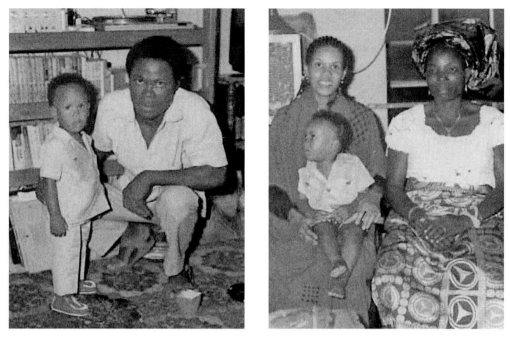

Above left: Me, with my uncle Samuel, one of my father's younger brothers.

Above right: Sitting on my mother's lap, next to my Auntie Rebecca, one of my father's older sisters.

Below: Hanging with my siblings at a house party in Lagos. That's my brother Joseph on the far left, seated next to Johnson. My little sister, Melissa, is sitting on the lap of my big sister, Malinda, and then there's me leaning up against my brother Anthony. (Our brother Justin, the baby of the family, wasn't born until we moved to the States a couple years later.)

All photos courtesy of Alex Owumi.

Above left: Me, on my birthday. Check out my Good Humor Man shoes.

Above right: A formal shot of me and my brother Anthony. I'm the handsome dude up top.

Below: We look like trouble, don't we? *Left to right:* me, Johnson, Anthony, Joseph, and Melissa in front.

Above: The Al-Nasr Benghazi starting five: *left to right:* Moustapha Niang, Alaa Elmansouri, me, Ibrahim Mohammed, and Abdul Rahim.

Right and below: Here I am bringing up the ball for El-Olympi in the Egyptian League and calling a play in a close game down the stretch.

At a surprise birthday party with my El-Olympi teammates. For a time in there, I didn't think I'd make it to 27.

Left: Views from my rooftop in Benghazi.

Below: The view from my living room. Note the charred facade of the police headquarters building across the way.

Above and below: Waiting, waiting, waiting at the border patrol in Sallum. We were there for three days before ducking out in the middle of the night.

Left: Kissing the championship trophy in Cairo.

Below: As you can see, I didn't want to let go of that thing on the bus ride home.

All cleaned up for a night on the town with Alexis to celebrate our one-year anniversary.

FIVE | SKOPJE

HERE IS WHERE THINGS went off the rails.

Not too long after I met Alexis and things started to get serious between us, I got a call from my agent telling me he'd received an offer from KK Lirija Skopje, a team in the Macedonian Super-league. The money was nice—about $10,000 per month, plus expenses—and it turned out I knew a little about the league, because I had a couple of buddies over there.

Basketball's like anything else. Spend a bunch of time in that world and it gets smaller and smaller. By this point I'd been at it so long, played on so many different teams with so many different clubs, trained in so many different clinics, that it was starting to feel like I'd played with or against just about everybody. I could travel halfway around the planet and still run into a guy I knew from some gym back home.

It wasn't such a big surprise that I got this offer from Macedonia, because my agent was Macedonian—born and raised, in fact. His name was Goran Gramatikov, and I'd met him in the States. He went to school in Florida, so his English was close enough to perfect, but he lived in Macedonia part of the year. He had a lot of basketball connections there, and when he took me on after I got back from France, he mentioned this as a possibility. He'd sent a lot of players to Macedonia, he said, and many of them stayed on for more than just one season, which was always a good barometer.

If you're happy, you stay; if you're not, you leave.

I didn't have a whole lot of options in the States, and I wasn't too psyched about returning to the Millrats without Rob Spon around to coach, so I had to consider it. I hated the idea of leaving Alexis behind in the States, though. We'd only been "together" four or five months, even though we weren't always in the same city, and yet I think we both knew we could survive a few months apart. Still, Macedonia seemed like a world away, the great unknown. I suppose I could have reached back out to my contacts in the French league, maybe returned for another season, or maybe tried to latch on to a D-League team, but I thought it made sense to mix things up, put myself out there in front of as many different folks as possible who might be in a position to help me down the road. I hate to sound so scheming, so calculating, but that had to be my mind-set just then. I had to keep building on that long list of basketball connections. I had to look at every opportunity, not just for the chance it offered for me to earn a decent paycheck and to keep playing, but to push myself forward. I had to think, *Okay, I've done the France thing; so now what?*

I'd been told they play a tough brand of basketball in Macedonia. That was cool with me. That's how I grew up playing, so I didn't mind a little rough-and-tumble, a few elbows. That was my game. So I talked it over with my family—with my girlfriend, basically—just to talk myself into going. I wanted to get Goran's

take, too, thinking he was closer to the situation than anyone I
could dig up on my own, and he had mostly positive things to
say. He laid it all out for me, the good and the bad, but the bottom line was that he had a couple of clients over there already,
including some on their second "tour," so I took this as a positive
and started to lean towards signing. I guess I needed a little extra
push, you know, and while we were all talking it through, I
opened up my laptop and started checking out the region online.
I didn't know too much about that part of the world, but I was
a quick study. I liked that Macedonia was right next to Greece, a
place I'd always wanted to visit. I liked that it'd be a chance to
try out a whole other culture, a whole new mess of foods, a
new way of looking out at the world. I was a little put off by the
language, because I didn't think I'd ever heard anyone speak
Macedonian, but according to Wikipedia, a lot of folks over there
also spoke Turkish and English, in addition to a bunch of other
Slavic languages, so I figured I'd get by. It wouldn't be like it was
in France, where everyone seemed to speak a little English,
where I could understand a little French, but I'd manage.

I don't think I really considered the differences I'd encoun-
ter between Eastern and Western Europe. Despite my world
travels, I wasn't exactly a world traveler. Yeah, I'd grown up in
Nigeria, but I'd never left Lagos until we moved out of the
country. Yeah, we spent some time in London, but only in a
just-passing-through sort of way, as we made our way across the
Atlantic to Boston. And yeah, I'd played in the French league
for a season, but I'd been so busy playing ball, I didn't see a
whole lot of France. To me, just then, Europe was Europe—only
Skopje, Macedonia, turned out to be nowhere near as nice as

Antibes had been, nowhere near as nice as Paris or any of the other French cities where we'd played. Skopje had a kind of run-down feel, but I didn't notice it at first. I was distracted by the enthusiastic greeting I got at the airport. Apparently, it made the newspapers that Lirija had just signed a new international player, and there had been a couple of articles about me before I even arrived. They started calling me Alexander the Great, which I've got to admit was a kick-ass nickname—obvious, I guess, given my first name, but I wasn't expecting it. I remembered enough high school history to know that Alexander the Great was this ancient king of the Macedon region who'd once ruled over one of the largest empires in the world, so I didn't mind the name at all. That's what they called the airport, too, so it was pretty surreal, landing at Alexander the Great Airport and hearing all these chants, people holding up signs welcoming "Alexander the Great," calling out my new name.

I heard that and thought, *Okay, these people are cool.* I thought, *This place will be just fine.* And as far as any language barrier, I thought I understood the locals well enough. Alexander the Great, man . . . What else did I need to know?

It turned out I needed to know plenty. And this became clear right away, on the cab ride from the airport to my hotel. I'd exchanged a little bit of money as I was racing through the air-port, but I hadn't really figured out the currency yet, and I was still sorting all those numbers in my head when I hailed a cab—an ancient, beat-up Volkswagen Golf. I told the driver where I was headed, and I think I knew in the back of my mind that it should have been about a $10 fare, but when he dropped me off,

I started handing the driver some money and saying, "Is this okay? Is this okay?"

I'd hand him a bill, and he'd shake his head and keep his palm out, like he was telling me it wasn't enough, so I took this guy at his word and kept giving him more and more money. It never even occurred to me that the driver might rip me off. Either I was a little too trusting or way too naive. In my defense, I'd just been greeted at the airport by this wave of good cheer, so I had no reason to think all of Macedonia wouldn't be super-friendly and welcoming, but this asshole cab driver was happy to see me for a whole other reason. Basically, I had no idea what I was doing, and this cabbie knew I had no idea what I was doing, and he took me for $70 or $80, just for that one short ride. I figured it out after the driver had pulled away, and the whole rest of the time I was in Skopje, I was on the lookout for that crappy VW. I don't know what I would have done if I came across it, but I hated that I'd been burned like that as soon as I got into town.

One of the hardest adjustments to playing ball in Macedonia was getting used to the fact that they don't heat the arenas. It was the strangest thing. They play in these nice, relatively new venues, some of them seating up to eight or ten thousand, but apparently they save money by dialing down the heat. The idea is that once the fans pile in, all that body heat will warm the place up, and it usually does, but it takes a long time. In the dead of winter, when we stepped onto the court for a pregame shoot-around, it could be twenty degrees in there, Fahrenheit. It was insane, bizarre. We couldn't feel our fingers. The maintenance guys would put a steel trash can on the floor behind the basket, and we'd get a fire going, try to chase the feeling back into our fingers. We'd go through our warm-up wearing hats and gloves, hoodies and jackets. It's like we were dressed for ice hockey, not basketball. It took about an hour just to break a sweat, so it was almost impossible to start a game feeling good and ready to play. The local guys were used to conditions like this, but it gave me some trouble. Some nights I'd score fifteen, sixteen points and wonder what kind of numbers I would have put up if I'd hit the ground running.

It was all bare bones, reminded me a lot of Alcorn State.

There were three other Americans on the team—Chucky Frierson, Jerry Cheves, and Richard Jeter. We all lived in the same neighborhood, in a part of Skopje that was mostly Albanian. When I got there, I didn't know enough to know what that might mean. The team put us up in a fleabag hotel, one of those places that look and sound and smell like they rent rooms by the hour to local prostitutes, so there were all kinds of sketchy-looking types coming and going from our building at all hours. I didn't know what that might mean, either, except there was always a lot of noise, a lot of yelling and screaming, a lot of doors slamming in the middle of the night. Sometimes it sounded like my neighbors were moving around all of their furniture, and then, the next day, at around the same time, they'd move all of it around again. I'd be on the computer, on Skype, talking to Alexis back home, and she'd have to listen to all this noise in the background. She kept saying, "What the hell is that? What the hell is *that?*"

Clearly, our living situation left a little something to be desired, but even worse was the fact that we were surrounded by all these Muslims who just weren't used to seeing black people, not at all. We stood out, man. And it's not just because we were a little too tall—no, it's because we were a little too black. The part of Skopje where we were living, where we played our games, was pretty damn racist. A heads-up would have been nice—because absolutely, this was something my agent would have known, something he should have shared. People just stared at us everywhere we went. In our neighborhood it was mostly benign, mostly nothing, but even so it was annoying. It got in the way, left us feeling like we were on display. Mostly, it kept us from enjoying ourselves when we weren't playing ball, kept us from hanging out in the clubs, unless we were all together, in case something went down. Nothing ever happened, but then after a while, what started out as nothing got a little ugly, a little hateful. It followed us onto the court as well. We'd play games in other parts of the country, and when we'd start to run up the score, the fans would turn on us. They'd start calling us niggers, monkeys, gorillas. They spoke Slavic, but somehow they knew the word *nigger.* Somehow they knew *gorilla.* They learned it from American rap songs, apparently. From American movies. In one gym, we took the court, and there was this whole section of assholes, standing and pointing and shouting, "Ku Klux Klan! Ku Klux Klan!"

It's amazing, alarming, the way that kind of shit travels.

The worst of it came against one of our rivals, Rabotnicki. That team was also based in Skopje, and we were beating up on them pretty good. At least that's how the game started out. We were in second place heading into this game, and they were in third place, so even though it was early in the season, it was set up to be an intense game, and the arena was packed. But the

Rabotnicki fans weren't typical fans. They were terrible, almost like animals. I don't know that it's fair to generalize, because it might have been just a small percentage of fans doing us dirt, but I'll go ahead and generalize anyway. They were all animals as far as I was concerned. We had a couple of Albanian players on our team, and some idiots in the crowd held up an Albanian flag and set fire to it. Right in the middle of the game. Not to keep warm, to feed the fire in the garbage can by the basket, but to piss our guys off. Then they started throwing shit down on the floor—water bottles, cups, food—whatever they could find. Rocks, even. They spat on one or two of our guys. It was like a madhouse, and it rattled our side pretty good, to where the Rabotnicki players started to turn things around.

We'd had a nice momentum going until momentum seemed not to matter. Also, I'd been having a strong game to this point, until that didn't matter, either. With about five minutes to go in the game, I'd scored about twenty points, but then the fans got even worse. Play was stopped momentarily. All this garbage started to rain down on us, all these horrible taunts, and my Albanian teammates finally just snapped. They went a little nuts.

You know all those famous stories about how Branch Rickey used to sit with Jackie Robinson and go over how the Dodgers expected Jackie to respond to the racism he'd face as the first black baseball player? The way he was supposed to keep his cool and let the assaults and insults slide? Well, these Albanian kids weren't like that. Not even close. They started to run up into the stands—right in the middle of the run of play—I guess thinking they'd beat the crap out of these racist assholes, maybe catch them by surprise. They didn't get very far before another one of our teammates hurled a glass bottle into the crowd in frustration, and that kicked the chaos up to a whole other level. The bottle hit some poor kid on the side of the head, and at that point the chaos spilled all the way over into a full-blown riot. Both teams were in the stands, fighting. There were fans on the court, fighting. The police had to come in to break it all up. It took more than two hours to clear the place out, and the kicker was that we never finished the game. Some league official decided it was unsafe to continue, and since Rabotnicki had inched ahead at the time of the brawl, they were awarded the win.

The incident reminded me of that famous brawl in Detroit in 2004, in that game between the Pistons and the Indiana Pacers— "the Malice at the Palace." It was that bad. In fact, it might have been worse.

I got back to my room that night thinking I'd had enough. I mean, this was some wild, loopy shit. This was dangerous. This was so completely not what I'd signed on for. So I got Goran Gramatikov on the phone and told him to get me the hell out of there. Told him to find me another place to play. Told him I'd rather go home than stay on in this environment.

Later that night, my American teammates decided to head out to a club. In Skopje, everyone called it a disco, but I wasn't up to joining them at first. I was still shaken by what had just gone down in the arena. I wanted to talk to Goran back home. I wanted to talk to Alexis and get her take, too, but after a while I was feeling cooped up in my room and decided to join my friends. The problem, though, was that the guys had already left, and we weren't in the habit of traveling around town without each other for support. Still, I told myself it was no big deal to grab a cab on my own and meet up with them, so that's what I set out to do.

A couple of blocks from the disco, I passed an ATM machine. I was low on cash, so I asked the driver to let me out, told him I'd walk the rest of the way. Even the driver didn't think this was such a good idea. He shrugged and scrunched up his face, like he was asking me if I was sure. It was after midnight in a mostly deserted part of town in the middle of a dark street.

I wasn't sure of anything, but I figured I'd be okay. I signaled to the driver that I was cool, that everything was under control. So he took off, and almost as soon as I saw his taillights disappear around the next corner, I regretted it. Before I even got to the ATM, I saw this odd, menacing-looking kid come skulking towards me. The fact that he struck me as being so menacing was probably the oddest part of the whole deal, because the kid was only eight or nine years old. I'd seen him around town, I thought, usually with a bunch of other menacing-looking kids around the same age. We called them jackals. They traveled in packs, like gypsies, terrorizing the good, law-abiding people of Skopje who were stupid enough to walk the streets of the city alone. This one wore an eye patch—I could see from across the street—but then as he got closer, I noticed he was carrying a baby girl. This might seem strange, but it really wasn't, because one of the big scams run by these jackals was to approach you in the street with a baby and try to tug at your heartstrings a little bit. They'd point to the baby, indicate that they were hungry, ask for money. And that's just what this kid with the eye patch was doing here. He crossed the street to where I was standing. He pointed to the baby, drew his fingers to his mouth and pinched them together to show that he was hungry. Then he said, "Money! Money! Money!"

It was dark where I was standing—like, scary dark. I was caught off guard, but only a little. And then, from around the corner, another four or five jackals came from behind doorways, alleys . . . whatever. It's like they burst onto the scene out of nowhere. They descended on me fast. One of them carried what looked to be a tire iron, and he ran right up to me and started swinging it like a maniac. Hit me pretty damn hard, too.

I took off. Just fisted my ATM money in my pockets and took off.

These kids were tiny, came up to my waist. But there were five or six of them. And soon there were a couple more. So I ran. I didn't think they'd take off after me, but they did. Even the kid with the baby gave chase. He just kind of tucked the baby under his arm like a football and started running. I ran for about a half mile, all the way to the front door of the disco, and when I reached the sign out front and a crowd of other people, the jackals finally dispersed.

I was gassed when I found my friends, just inside the door. And pissed. I hated that these little kids had made me so afraid. Plus I was frantic, excited. My leg was banged up pretty good, but I was on an adrenaline high, and a part of me wanted to go back out after the kids, maybe throw a scare at them, for payback. So I told my friends what just happened, told them I'd just been jumped stepping away from the ATM machine. Told them there were about five or six of them.

One of my friends said, "Who jumped you?"

I said, "Some little jackals."

My friends, they knew all about these jackals. They knew they were only eight or nine years old. They knew they only came up to my waist. So they laughed and laughed, like it was the funniest thing in the world, me running from a pack of wild kids. And I guess to them it was pretty damn funny, the thought of me running through the dark, empty streets after midnight, chased by a little boy with an eye patch carrying a baby.

Me, I didn't think it was so damn funny.

I'd remain in Skopje another couple of days, but I never played another game for Lirija. I'd seen enough.

———ɯ———

The very next morning, Goran called with a new prospect. I hadn't expected him to move so quickly, but it worked out that he got a call from another agent who was trying to find players of African descent willing to play in Libya. I fit the profile, Goran said. I was from Nigeria. I'd had some international experience. And I was able to travel immediately. Goran said he could get me out of my Lirija contract, no problem. So I told him I'd do it. Just like that, without really thinking about it, I asked him to set it up.

I didn't even ask about the terms of the deal, not on that first call. The money was usually about the same—or close enough that I didn't want to base my decision on money. My expenses would be covered, and the money I'd earn would be more than I could make back home, so it really wasn't an issue. Anyway, I couldn't stand the idea of staying in Skopje any longer than I had to, so I jumped at the chance to bolt. Before Goran could get back to me with any details, though, I reached out on Skype to tell Alexis the good news.

I said, "There's a team in Libya that wants me to come play for them."

She said, "Libya? How'd that happen?"

I told her I'd asked my agent to find me another place to stay, told her about the brawl, the burning of the Albanian flag. She'd already heard about the racism and the taunts and the hate-filled crap the fans would shout at us. I filled her in on what had happened the night before. Told her about the riot at the arena, about getting jumped at the ATM by those wild gypsy kids. I said, "This place is miserable."

And it was. It truly was. But Alexis had a sick, uncertain feeling that Libya might be even worse. She couldn't say why exactly, only that she wanted to spend some time looking into it. She made me promise I wouldn't commit to anything until I heard back from her—so, of course, I promised. Remember, it was just five years since Hurricane Katrina, since she'd lost everything back home in New Orleans, and she wasn't about to keep quiet if another someone she loved was about to step into some other disaster area.

A couple of hours later, she called me back, sounding a little panicked. She said, "Don't do it, Alex. I don't think Libya's the best place for you to be."

Apparently she'd hopped on to Google, read everything she could about the region. This was December 2010—the very beginning of a period of revolution and unrest that would come to be known as the Arab Spring. It would start in Tunisia, which bordered Libya to the northwest. Then it would spread to Egypt, which bordered Libya to the east. Then to the south in Sudan.

And on and on. Alexis didn't know any of this just yet, because it wasn't really being talked about, written about. It was just getting under way. Already, just that past week on the streets of Tunisia, there'd been a wave of protests calling for the resignation of president Zine El-Abidine Ben Ali, who'd been in power for nearly a quarter century, but Alexis didn't have her ear that close to the ground.

All she could learn, really, was that the region was at some kind of boiling point, and she was afraid there'd be antigovernment protests in Libya before long. She didn't like what she read about Qaddafi, she said. The White House didn't trust him. She thought Libya was a revolution just waiting to happen.

She said, "It's not safe, Alex. Come home." Underneath, what I heard her saying was "It's just like the hurricane all over again. You have to see it coming."

I didn't know how to respond to this. A part of me wanted to be a good boyfriend, to do the responsible, caring thing and give her no cause to worry. And if Alexis was worrying, then I could be damn sure she'd have my mother worrying, too. But another part of me just wanted to play ball. I didn't want to be stupid, didn't want to put myself in danger, but I didn't see any real danger here. Of course, all I knew of Libya was what I'd known growing up in Nigeria. In my little-kid memory, Colonel Muammar Qaddafi was no tyrant. He was the king of kings. His government sent a lot of money to our country. There were Libyan-backed relief efforts all over Africa. Tripoli was like Washington, in my mind. It was the seat of power on the continent, the place where all of the important decisions got made, where the interests of the people were served. No, I hadn't really kept up on the news since we'd left Nigeria. I had no clue, really, what was going on over there. I was only pointing to some decades-old image I'd had of Qaddafi and Libya that was probably a distorted picture even when I was a kid. I told myself that Libya had been stable then and was stable now, same as it ever was.

Alexis knew, though. She had, like, a sixth sense about this. She felt it in her bones, she said—but it wasn't just instinct that got her thinking this way. No, she was realizing what the rest of the world was also just now realizing—that the Internet had given the people a voice, and they were using it to bring about change, to end years and years of oppressive treatment. Alexis saw no reason for me to put myself in the middle of that change.

She said, "Just come home, Alex. You can find a place to play here."

I also spoke to my brothers and my parents, and they all kind of sided with Alexis. They weren't as plugged in to what was going on over there, but they didn't trust Qaddafi, either. They believed his regime was like a stick of dynamite and that the fuse had been lit. They wanted me home.

But I just wanted to play ball—and, since I was in midseason shape, I wanted to land with a team that would put me on the floor right away. I didn't want to lose another year to some vague idea of political unrest that might or might not have any-thing to do with where I was going. I hated to go against Alexis's wishes, especially after what she'd been through, but even more than that, I would have hated staying away for no good reason. I was young enough and stupid enough and arrogant enough and probably provincial enough to think that if the situation in Libya changed, if the seeds of protest and unrest started to grow, I'd have plenty of time to get my ass out of there. I'd be totally in control.

So I waited for Goran to get back to me with final details, not knowing what I'd tell him when he called. Either I was in or I was out; I would see.

—⁕—

I was in, of course. The money was too good to pass up—almost twice what I'd been making in Macedonia, the kind of money that could carry me for the next while. And Goran had set it up so I could travel to Benghazi and be ready to play my first game before the end of the week.

Alexis wasn't too happy with me, but she knew that once I set my mind to a thing, I wasn't going to turn back. She'd made her point. My family had, too. They'd made their separate pitches for me to come home, and they even ganged up on me and made a kind of tag-team pitch, but I'd decided to stay. Libya was Libya. I'd known that place my whole life. Qaddafi was Qaddafi. Nothing had changed. It felt to me like nothing was about to change, either. It felt to me like I was in control, like it was no big deal.

Before I left, Alexis called me up one last time to try and talk me out of my decision. She said she'd had a vision. One thing you need to know about my girl is that she has these visions—feelings, premonitions, dreams—whatever you want to call them. She swears by them, and if I had known what was good for me, I would have sworn by them, too.

She said, "I had a dream last night, Alex."

I thought, *Oh, no. Here we go.*

She told me about her dream. There was a lot of fog, she said. People were dying. It was tough to make out what she was seeing, exactly, because of all that fog, but it creeped her out. It reminded her of a painting. It was dark and eerie and otherworldly. In her dream she could hear people screaming, which didn't sound to me like any damn painting I'd ever seen.

She said, "It means you should come home. Something's not right."

I said, "No, it means you had a weird dream. Everything's all right. You'll see."

We were both stubborn, dug in. But this was something I wanted. This was something close at hand, easy enough. This was good money. Again, I hated to go against Alexis, to go against my family. I can't stress that enough. But at the same time, I think I hated the idea of caving in to what I felt was a vague, unsupported fear even more.

The next morning, I was packed and ready to go. The plan was to catch a cab to the airport for a flight to Budapest, Hungary. It turned out there was no good way to get from Skopje to Benghazi, but someone in the office of my new Libyan team made all the arrangements. The team offering the contract was Al-Nasr Benghazi, and they were one of the top teams in Libya's D1 league. They had a ton of money, Goran said. The way it worked in Libya was that the professional sports clubs were owned by the government. That's how it works in a lot of countries, only in Libya, many teams were also privately run, through a special arrangement with the government. Here, Goran said, the team was subsidized by a very important Libyan family, but that was all he shared with me at this point. Maybe that's because this was all he knew, and I didn't ask for any details. What the hell did I care who they were, so long as they paid me? In any case, someone in the Al-Nasr office made all my travel plans for me, so I had no reason to think there'd be any kind of hassle. And there wouldn't have been, except for the weather. Almost as soon as I got in the cab, the driver turned back and said the airport was closed. He said, "No flights in, no flights out." The city was socked in with fog, and I didn't make the connection just then to Alexis's dream from the night before. It was just one of those things, I thought, so I went back to my hotel to wait out the weather.

The day after that, it was the same thing—fog. Same thing the next day, too. It was ridiculous. And it's not like the weather was so bad you couldn't fly through it. Back home in Boston, Logan Airport would have been open for business. But here in Skopje, the Alexander the Great Airport was completely shut down.

Finally, I called my agent and said, "You've got to get me out of here, man."

He suggested I take a train to Greece, and then fly from there to Jordan and then on to Libya, so I thought, *Why didn't you tell me this yesterday?* I said, "The team will pay for this, too?"

He said, "The team will pay."

The train station in Skopje was filthy, disgusting. I'd never seen anything like it. There were rats everywhere—big, mean-looking rats all over everything, every which way. Cockroaches, too—like giant water bugs, dozens of them, everywhere you looked. I thought I'd be sick, and then when I got on the train, I thought I'd be sicker still. The cars were also filled with rats and cockroaches, only here in this tight, small space, it was much harder to take. Your knees were jammed against the knees of the person sitting across from you. You were squeezed tight into the seats—that is, if you could even sit. I actually had to stand most of the way, which was just as well, because at least it put a little distance between me and all that mangy-looking, nasty-ass vermin crawling around the floor, on the seats, all over.

I was on that train for seven hours. That's how long it takes to get from Skopje to Thessaloniki, Greece, even though it's less than a couple hundred miles. From there it's another seven hours to Athens, but I had to wait until the next morning to set out. I had to sleep on a bench at the Thessaloniki train station, which sucked big time. The good news was that the connecting train was halfway decent. And the Athens train station was really nice—like, gorgeous. Coming from the station in Skopje, it felt like it was out of a different century. The city itself was beautiful. It was Christmas Eve when I pulled into town, so most of Athens was shut down. The streets were mostly empty. The restaurants were closed. I was lucky to find a hotel. Actually, I was superlucky because the hotel was great. It cost only one hundred euros a night, and the place was done up with all this old-world charm.

I hadn't really considered the calendar when I made my travel plans. Since it was Christmas Eve, I soon learned, I'd have to stay in Athens a second night, too, because my connecting flight wasn't until December 26. This was also just as well, I thought. If I had to be stuck in some city far from home on Christmas, I couldn't have picked a better spot. I walked the streets for a couple of hours, felt like I had the city all to myself. I thought, *Why the hell can't I play here?* There's a Greek league, there's a team in Athens. Yeah, the Greek economy was shit.

Yeah, there was probably just as much chance of an uprising here as there might be in Libya, but to walk those deserted streets on Christmas Eve, you'd never have guessed there was a debt crisis or anything like that. You'd never have guessed that the whole country was at a boiling point, that the economy or the government could come toppling down at any time. The trains were still running in and out of that beautiful station. There were nice hotels, shops, restaurants. I told myself I should get on Goran to hook me up with an Athenian team for next season.

I got up late the next morning and kind of hung out for a bit in my room, waiting for my girlfriend's family to wake up back home, waiting for my own family to wake up. The plan was to open our presents together on Skype so I could feel like a part of their Christmas. This was kind of a pathetic way to spend the holiday, except when we got down to it, I didn't mind it at all. Actually, it was kind of nice to be so connected to the people I loved, from so far away. It made me think what a cool world we lived in. It's amazing, really, the way technology lets us keep our world small, within reach, and we abused the crap out of the technology that Christmas. I thought the people from Skype, they should hire us to advertise their service, because we were all over it, man. We were like the poster family for Skype. All day long, I kept checking in with Alexis or with my family, so it felt a little bit like I was hanging with them. Not a lot, but a little, which would have to be enough. The rest of the time, I watched movies on my laptop. *Beverly Hills Cop, Rush Hour 3* . . . no Christmas movies, though. Just whatever comedy-adventure movies I had on my computer. Just whatever I could find to keep myself amused.

I was basically twiddling my thumbs, waiting for Christmas

to pass so I could continue on my way. The deal was I'd have to fly to Amman, Jordan, and then there'd be, like, a two-hour layover for my connecting flight to Libya. Only the layover turned out to be way longer than two hours. There was a problem with my visa, I was told. Either it wasn't ready or it hadn't been filled out properly. The people at the airport weren't exactly helpful. All they could tell me was that I would have to wait and wait and wait. The first plane I was supposed to catch took off without me. Then the next one took off without me. After six or seven hours, someone from the airline, Royal Jordanian, told me I'd have to wait until the next afternoon before I could fly and suggested I find a comfortable place to sleep in the terminal.

I thought, *Are you shittin' me?*

I found someone from the airline who spoke passable English and I said, "Look, somebody paid a lot of money for my plane ticket. Over a thousand U.S. dollars. I shouldn't have to sleep on the floor."

I went back and forth about this with a whole bunch of people, until I finally found some airline higher-up who agreed to make a couple of calls on my behalf. She came back and told me the airline had agreed to put me up in a hotel, so I followed that person's directions to where a cab was supposed to be waiting for me outside. The whole time, I was thinking I'd go to some nice-enough hotel in the city a couple of miles from the airport, but the cab driver kept driving and driving. He didn't speak a lick of English, and outside my window, the scenery was going from a nice, modern city to a real slum. We drove for, like, fifteen, twenty minutes, and it's like we went from prosperity to poverty in a blink. It was a little scary, wherever we were.

Then, without a word, the driver pulled to a stop in just about the worst part of town we'd been to so far. He got out and walked around to the back of the cab, grabbed my bags, and set them on the dirt road. I had a single suitcase and a giant duffel, and he just dropped them down and stood behind them, waiting for me to open the passenger door and get out. I was stunned, didn't really know what to do, but I stepped cautiously out of the car and was met by a guy who'd come out of the nearest building to collect my bags. Before I could figure out who this new guy was or what was happening, the cabbie ducked back into his car and sped away, leaving me alone on this dirt street in front of what looked more like a house than a hotel.

The guy who'd been left with my bags was nice enough. His English was okay. I followed him inside, past a dingy front desk. The place was like a small rooming house in need of a paint job, a thorough cleaning, and some new furniture. I couldn't imagine how it was that the airline had sent me here, instead of to one of the bigger, finer hotels near the airport, but I was stuck. Also, I was hungry. I hadn't eaten since Athens, I was now realizing, and I was starting to feel a little light-headed. So I asked the guy for something to eat.

He said, "No problem."

Then I asked if there was wireless, and he looked at me like I'd just made up a new word. "Internet," I explained.

"No," he said. "No Internet."

"Phone?" I asked.

"No," he said. "No phone."

"What about a SIM card for my cell phone?" I tried.

Again he looked at me strangely, so I held out my cell phone and poked stupidly at the touch screen, trying to show him that I wanted to find a way to make it work.

"No," he said, understanding at last. "No SIM card."

My room was horrible. The bed was unmade, the wallpaper was peeling, the faucet ran brown water. And yet despite all of this, the guy with the bags moved around the room like he was showing me the presidential suite.

He said, "Whatever you do, Mr. Alex, do not go outside. If you leave, if something happen, no one will know where you are."

This struck me as an odd thing to say to a guest checking in to a hotel. Also, it made no sense. Already no one knew where I was. My phone didn't work. I hadn't spoken with anyone back home since I'd left for Jordan. My girlfriend, my family, my agent—they were all probably out of their heads by now trying to figure out what the hell had happened to me, why I hadn't checked in with them yet.

A couple of minutes later, the bag guy came back with some water and crackers. The water was bottled, so I could safely drink it, but the crackers were spread out on a paper plate. They tasted like cardboard, but I ate them anyway, and as he was leaving the guy said, "That is all for the food. You eat too fast, there is no more."

Again, I didn't understand this. Did it mean there was nothing else to eat in all of Amman? Nothing else to eat in this room?

And then, just to leave me even more confused, the guy repeated his warning from before. He said, "Do not leave. It is not safe. If something happen, no one will know."

I locked the door behind him—that's how freaked I was by his warning, by this strange scene—and to pass the time, I started watching movies on my laptop. I actually watched *Rush Hour 3* for the second time in two days, because that shit just cracks me up. I needed to laugh in the worst way. After that I watched *The Book of Eli*, which is probably one of my all-time favorite movies. I'd seen it maybe a hundred times, no exaggeration, and each time I took something new from it. Each time I'd see myself as Denzel Washington. I survived the Apocalypse, and there's one copy of the Bible remaining in all of civilization, and it's in my head, committed to memory, and it falls on me to recite it, word for word, so scribes can take it down and send it all back out into the world. No matter how many times I watch that movie, it always hits me like something brand-new, and here it got me thinking to pull out my own Bible. I'd taken to carrying a little green edition, put out by Gideons International, and I opened it to the book of Genesis. This alone wasn't so unusual. I read the Bible all the time, but I tended to just dive in here and there, maybe skip to Psalms or Corinthians. But this time I thought to start at the beginning. I don't know why, but I got it in my head to open to the first page and start reading. In the back of my mind, I was thinking I might just read all the way through on this trip to Libya. It would be a way to keep myself focused, but as I read, I drifted off. I didn't exactly sleep, but I closed my eyes. I listened to the strange noises coming up from the dirt streets outside my window, wondering how the hell I'd landed in such a funky, frightening place. And how the hell long I'd have to stay there.

—◊—

It took about a day and a half for my visa to be okayed by Libyan authorities, and once that finally happened, someone sent a cab to collect me from my crappy hotel. I'd taken the bag guy's advice and stayed holed up in my room the entire time, afraid to venture out on the mean streets in that part of Amman, so I hadn't really had anything to eat for more than twenty-four hours, just some water and a couple more crackers and some stale Boreo cookies, which were really just off-brand Oreos.

The good news was that Al-Nasr had set me up with a first-class ticket from Amman to Benghazi—or maybe some kind soul at Royal Jordanian took pity on me and gave me an upgrade. The flight was the first taste of comfort and luxury I'd had since I'd left for Macedonia about a month earlier, so I tried to really enjoy myself. I got to eat some real food, finally. I got to sleep without worrying about strange doings outside my hotel room door. Unfortunately, it was a short flight, so my vacation was over almost as soon as it started.

I was met at the airport by the Al-Nasr team president, Ahmed Elturki, who looked a little too much like Danny DeVito's Penguin character from *Batman Returns* in size and shape. As soon as I saw him and made the connection, I had to try not to laugh, but he gave me a really nice welcome. He told me he'd been waiting for me a good long time and that there were a lot of people anxious to meet me.

I wasn't sure what he meant by that, but I found out soon enough.

There was no real baggage-claim area, just a spot in the dirt by the runway where they set out your bags, so we walked over and grabbed my suitcase and duffel and continued on along the dirt runway and then through the airport. Mr. Ahmed walked me past a gauntlet of guards, their rifles resting against their shoulders, their faces locked in tough and menacing scowls. Only when they looked at me, the guards seemed to smile a bit, like they were happy to see me. I thought that was pretty weird, and it caught me by surprise. And then, as we kept walking, we could see all these fans just bunched up and waiting for me, it turned out. They were all wearing green—the team's colors, the country's colors. My plane was a couple of hours late, but these people had been waiting and waiting, I found out. A lot of them stepped from the crowd to greet me. One woman gave me some food. Someone else gave me a hat and a team jacket. Also weird. Also surprising. But it was also pretty damn cool, and nothing at all like the reception I'd gotten in Skopje. Mr. Ahmed explained that my signing was a big story in the local newspapers and on television. There'd been footage from my games shown on Al Jazeera. He said, "The team has many fans. They are excited to see the new American superstar."

As we walked to our car, Mr. Ahmed filled me in a little more on the team, on his role, on what I could expect. He said, "I'm the one who talked to your agent."

I said, "Well, then it's nice to meet you. Happy to be here."

And just then, I was.

He said, "I have arranged a nice flat for you. I believe you will be pleased. Your agent said you wanted to be near the arena, near the practice facility. It has all been arranged."

I said, "Sounds great, man. Thank you."

Mr. Ahmed drove us through the city. He narrated along the way, told me what we were seeing, what I could expect, but I wasn't really listening. I was checking it out, though, and what was registering was a typical Middle Eastern city. In my mind I'd been picturing ancient structures, grand old palaces, historic statues and monuments, but outside my window there was just a lot of dirt and tumbledown buildings. Around every corner there seemed to be a bombed-out shell of a complex right next to a modern building in decent shape, but we seemed to be headed away from the nicer parts of the city. It was just like that ride from the airport in Amman, moving from nice enough to not nice at all.

This troubled me a little. Not enough to say anything, but enough to notice.

After a while, the driver turned onto one the narrowest, grubbiest streets I'd ever seen. In spots, it felt like it was barely wide enough to fit our car. The road had more potholes in it than a regular road, and every pothole was filled with muddy water. We'd landed at about noon, in the middle of a bright, sunny day, but here on this street there was only shadow. It's like we'd turned into another time zone, but at the same time, the street was filled with dozens of little kids playing soccer. The street was so tiny that the kids had to step to the side and press their backs against the buildings every time a car passed, but then they'd fall right back into playing, and dance and dribble around all those potholes like they were part of the game.

We rolled down this narrow street for a couple of blocks— Italy Street, or Shari Italioso—and then the taxi came to a sudden stop. Mr. Ahmed turned to me and said, "We are here."

I thought, *This is crazy. This can't be where I'm staying.* But just to be sure, I said, "We are where?"

He said, "This is your flat."

Mr. Ahmed could see from the expression on my face that I was disappointed, a little startled. I mean, the street where we were looked like some kind of back alley in a slum. So he moved to explain. He said, "You said you wanted to live close to the arena, close to downtown." He pointed, continued: "The arena is two blocks that way. Downtown is two blocks that way. The main square is just behind your building, on the other side. You can see it from your apartment window."

I said, "Okay, Mr. Ahmed. If you say so."

He stepped from the cab and said, "Come, you will see. I do not think you will be disappointed."

Then, as I stepped from the cab, a half-dozen kids who'd been playing soccer started swarming around me, jumping up and down. They couldn't speak any English, but they knew who I was. They were fans of Al-Nasr, and I could only guess that they'd seen me play on Al Jazeera, that they'd been expecting a tall black man to step from this very cab and turn around their season. One of them kicked a soccer ball to my feet, so I passed it back, and for a few joyful moments we were like children, playing soccer in the dirty water, laughing and jumping and having a big old time.

Ten minutes pass. Fifteen. It's possible I have drifted off. I am so completely spent, thrashed, disoriented. Really, I'm so beaten down by these past couple of hours that for another few moments, I have no clear recollection of how I've sunk to this spot on the floor, my back to the steel door. I do not know where I am, what I am doing.

Whatever noise has been coming in through the window, I can no longer hear it.

Whatever danger has been lurking outside my door, I can no longer sense it.

Whatever shit I'm in, I can no longer smell it.

Until I can. Until I do. Until I am startled back into ragged consciousness by another crush of noise, this time from the other side of my apartment door. I hear fighting—like, tussling, roughhousing kind of fighting. I hear shouting in Arabic. I hear screaming. For a beat I think it's nothing. It's like I am back in college, listening to a bunch of drunken idiots wrestle on the floor of my dormitory. I cannot place these noises or guess what they might mean, so I wait for the noises to quiet and open the door slowly. I do not want to be spotted, but at the same time I do not want to be stuck here on the wrong side of whatever the hell is going on in my hallway. I do not want to be powerless. I want to see what I can see, do what I can do, so I open the door a crack, and then a little bit more, and I peer through the slit opening. I can see diagonally into the hallway, but only a little, only a sliver over by the stairwell. Inside that sliver I can see the bloodied body of a man. The body is mostly still. There appears to be blood coming from the man's head. He is kind of moving, kind of not.

I know this man, I realize. I know his family. He lives down the hall. It is not such a big apartment building that we don't know each other, everyone on the same floor. We smile hello coming in and out of the elevator. We talk about the team, about the weather, about what's going on in Egypt. I know this man as Mr. Ashraf. Ashraf is his first name, but he introduced himself to me as Mr. Ashraf, so this is what I call him. I know his daughter, too. She's probably sixteen, seventeen—somewhere in there. Her name is Ariel. She speaks a little English, enough that we can communicate. She is a student, but I have no idea what she's studying, where she's studying. Perhaps she told me once, but I can't think straight. My thoughts are all over the place, on everything and nothing, all at once. Whatever I'm seeing, whatever is happening, it does not seem to fit together. I cannot comprehend that this bloodied body by the stairwell is the body of my neighbor Mr. Ashraf. I cannot accept that he is moving and not moving, all at once, that he is half dead right outside my front door. It makes no sense, him lying here, like this, in the middle of the hallway, in the middle of the day.

I would have heard a gunshot, I'm guessing. This is what I puzzle together in my racing mind. I think, Whatever happened to this man, it must have been hand to hand. *I think,* He must have been beaten, probably with the butts of those same AK-47s that pounded open my door. *I think,* Probably these soldiers know enough not to fire off their assault rifles in the confined space of an apartment stairwell.

I think, How the hell am I going to get out of here?

SIX | BENGHAZI

(Before)

MR. AHMED WAS RIGHT. I wasn't disappointed. The building itself was nice enough, although you wouldn't know it to step inside. The elevator was wild—no door, just a wire you had to pull across the threshold before the thing would go. The effect was a little unnerving, to be scrolling up past all these other floors, seeing all these people in the hallways outside their apartments, some of them looking, waving. There was nothing to do but look back and wave, too. When we reached the seventh floor, the top floor, we were met by a dozen or so of my new neighbors, who had apparently spilled from their apartments to check me out. Everyone was nodding in greeting. It was strange and at the same time kind of cool, but I still had an uneasy feeling about my apartment. I mean, the way all these people lived, hanging in the hallways, in the stairwells, playing in the dirty pothole water in the street out front, the place felt more like a tenement house than a luxury apartment building. But then I opened the heavy steel door to my apartment and was just blown away.

First of all, the door itself was just sick—like, ridiculously heavy. It reminded me of something you'd find in a bank vault, and as soon as we swung it open, I could understand why. The apartment just did not fit the building, the setting, the neighborhood, so it's like they needed that big steel door to keep the rest of Benghazi away. Like the only way to keep such a grand apartment in the middle of such a nothing-special building in a nothing-special neighborhood was to keep it shut away behind a tight, tight seal. The place was huge, gorgeous, done up with nice furniture and fine things. I thought, *Finally, a decent place to stay.* Only this was way better than decent. This was first class, off the hook—a three-bedroom penthouse—hell, yeah! The kitchen was outfitted with nice china and silverware and every type of pot and pan and cooking utensil I could ever hope to use. The designer-type couches were covered in stylish, high-end fabric. There was framed artwork on the walls. Nice carpeting. I'd never stayed in a place like this, not even for a single night in a high-end hotel, so I was psyched, man. I was pumped.

Mr. Ahmed saw me checking out the huge flat-screen television in the living room. He said, "We have satellite, over one thousand channels."

My eyes probably popped out of my head when I heard that. I thought, *Man, I don't ever have to leave this apartment. I could watch television all day.* I said, "What about NBA TV?"

As soon as I said that, I realized I sounded like a spoiled kid, but I *was* like a spoiled kid in a candy store, and I wanted it all.

He said, "If we don't have it, it can be arranged. Whatever you need, it can be arranged." Then he handed me a SIM card for my phone and about $500 worth of Libyan dinars, which was, like, my monthly stipend for groceries. He also gave me his phone number and the numbers for my coach and for the team office.

Then he left, telling me I should feel comfortable walking these streets, to get some rest, and that I needed to report to practice in two days.

It was December 27, 2010, a Monday, which gave me until Wednesday before I had to put on my gear and get to work. Already I'd been away from the gym for almost a week, so I was itching to get back to it, but at the same time I was looking forward to chilling in my new kick-ass apartment. I hadn't had a chance to really check the place out when Mr. Ahmed was there, so I started looking around, and right away I noticed a bunch of family-type photos that struck me as odd—also a little familiar. There, on a shelf by the television, was a group of framed photos of Colonel Qaddafi posing with a bunch of other people I didn't recognize. And there, on a table, was another group of photos of Qaddafi with a lot of the same people I now recognized from the first group. In some of the pictures, Qaddafi was a young man, the way I remembered him from all those news reports when I was a kid. In some he was younger still. And in others, in what I guessed were the most current shots, he looked a whole lot older.

I couldn't figure why this apartment was decorated with so many informal shots of the Libyan leader. It made no sense. For a beat or two, I thought maybe that was just the Libyan way, like how you'll sometimes see pictures of President Obama or President Bush in American households, or pictures of Jesus Christ or the pope in religious households.

I popped my new SIM card into my phone and made my first local call, to Ahmed Elturki. The man had said to call if I had any questions, any concerns, so here I was with my first question. I wasn't sure yet if it was also a concern.

I said, "Yo, Mr. Ahmed. What's with all these pictures of Colonel Qaddafi? They're all over the apartment."

He said, "Ah, yes. I did not mention. The apartment belongs to Mutassim Qaddafi, the colonel's son."

I said, "What's that about? Why would Colonel Qaddafi's son let me live in his great apartment? With all his stuff?"

He said, "Al-Nasr, it is the Qaddafi club. You are playing for the Qaddafi family. They want to make sure you are comfortable."

I thought, *Damn, what am I into here?*

Then I thought, *Damn, I'm hungry.*

I fired up my laptop and checked in quickly with my mother, with my girlfriend, just to let them both know I was safe and settled in my nice apartment. Then I rode back down that weird elevator in search of something to eat. I don't think I took the time just then to tell anyone back home who my landlord was, who my employers were, because a part of me didn't think anything of it. It was what it was—and yet, now that I knew this apartment belonged to Qaddafi's son, now that I knew I was playing for Qaddafi's team, the neighborhood didn't look half as depressing as it had on the way in. It's like the whole scene brightened, my whole outlook. Those same kids were still on the street out in front of my building, playing soccer, so I kicked the ball around with them for a couple of minutes and made my way to what looked like a small shopping area across the street. I passed a guy with a kind of food cart who was cooking up a batch of what I really, really hoped was chicken. It smelled amazing, and I was starving, so I grabbed a sandwich and tore into it. Oh, man, it was good. Like, crazy good. I don't know if it was because I hadn't eaten since the plane or if there was something special about the meat or the way it was seasoned or prepared, but I scarfed that thing down like it was some local delicacy.

Then, since I was out, I did some grocery shopping. I picked up a loaf of bread, some tuna, pasta, tomatoes, peppers . . . enough to hold me over for a day or so.

When I got back to my building, there was a cat by the door to my apartment, all the way up on the seventh floor. A black cat. I'm not superstitious or anything, but at the same time, I couldn't imagine what the hell a black cat was doing wandering around my hallway like that, so I left it alone. I shut the door behind me and started cooking, learning my way around the kitchen, whatever. As I cooked, as I looked through Mutassim Qaddafi's pots and pans and kitchen drawers, I kept hearing that cat meowing outside my front door. The poor thing must have been making some serious noise, because it traveled through that heavy steel door. So after a while of this I felt so bad for the animal that I went out to the hallway to feed it. It looked too healthy to be a stray, so I thought maybe he belonged to one of my new neighbors, but I fed him anyway. I put down the can of tuna, and he kind of leapt at it. I can't be sure, but I think I might have petted the cat, too, and then I went back inside and continued fixing myself something to eat. A short while later, the meowing stopped and I went back into the hallway, collected the empty can, and threw it in the trash. And again, I can't be sure if I petted the cat a second time (or maybe a first) or if I even washed my hands before going back to my food.

I mention these details because a couple of hours later, when

I was back on the computer talking to my girlfriend, filling her in on the whole Qaddafi connection, I started to feel violently ill. It hit me all of a sudden, just this overwhelming surge of cramps and nausea and discomfort. It felt to me like my body was going into shock, and the whole time this was happening, Alexis was staring back at me on Skype, wondering what was going on. She could see I wasn't looking right, and after a couple of beats, I doubled over in pain and she said, "Alex, you need to see a doctor."

I argued with her a time or two, told her it was nothing, just an upset stomach, but finally the pain was so unbearable, I agreed to call for the team doctor. Alexis stayed on chat while I dialed Ahmed Elturki again.

Two calls to the team president in less than two hours . . . I wondered if that made me one of his higher-maintenance players.

I said, "I'm sorry to bother you, Mr. Ahmed, but I'm in a lot of pain. I'm afraid something's wrong with my stomach."

He asked where I was, so I told him, and he promised to collect the team doctor and get there as quickly as possible. He said he was glad I'd called and happy to be of service. Fifteen minutes later, Mr. Ahmed knocked on my door with the team doctor, and almost as soon as I let them in, the team doctor said he'd need to get me to a hospital. He took one look at me doubled over in pain, looking like complete crap, and knew something was wrong.

Parasites. That was the team doctor's initial diagnosis, and it was confirmed by the doctors at the hospital in downtown Benghazi—which, by the way, was ultranice. Brand-new, state-of-the-art. I remember looking around as we rushed in and thinking it was so, so strange, that there was this spectacular hospital right in the middle of this ancient-looking city. The doctors there ran a bunch of tests, and then brought in a bunch of other doctors to consult. At first they were all saying the same thing, but then one of the doctors started talking about surgery. It was tough to follow because of the language, but this one doctor was saying that the only way to get rid of the parasites in my blood was to cut me open. And he wasn't just saying it, like it was just one opinion. No, he was saying it emphatically, like I could maybe die if I didn't have this operation.

I jumped in at this point. I said, "No way."

Mr. Ahmed was doing his best to translate for me, to keep me plugged in to what was going on, but it was a hectic scene, and it freaked me out to think these guys now wanted to perform surgery. I mean, the hospital was nice and all, but if I needed surgery, then I needed to get my ass back to the United States.

I said, "There must be some medication I can take, get rid of the parasites that way."

There was a lot of back-and-forth, a lot of talk I couldn't understand, but I made it clear that I wouldn't consent to surgery, so they came up with a course of medication I could try. One doctor said that without an operation, it could take two or three months for the medicine to clear all the parasites from my system. It wasn't clear if this was a best-case scenario or a worst-case scenario or just a plain-old scenario. Then another doctor said I should see an improvement in a couple of days. I thought that was a wide gap in diagnoses and decided to listen to the more hopeful doctor. I didn't see that I had any other choice, really, so they put me on a laxative and another drug called Antinal, a fairly common medication they give to a lot of travelers in that part of the world. With meds like that, I had the shits something fierce for days and days. And, not to be too gross or anything, but you could actually see these tiny parasites swimming around in the toilet, so they were trying to flush all of this out of me.

It was like a treading-water kind of deal. They had to pump me with enough fluids and electrolytes that I didn't waste away before I shit it all out. And then, when it looked to one of my doctors like I wasn't shitting these poisons out of my system fast enough, he induced vomiting by sticking some kind of instrument down my throat.

All in all, it wasn't the most pleasant hospital stay. They kept me for two days. The whole time, I couldn't really eat anything. I tried, but it'd just go right out the other end, so by the time they sent me back to my apartment, I was drained, exhausted. I was a little wobbly on my feet at first. I'd lost a bunch of weight. They'd managed to keep me from getting dehydrated, but I was dragging, man. I was aching all over, felt like I'd been left out in the sun for a couple of days with nothing to eat.

What sucked most about being in the hospital was that I couldn't call home. The team was good about passing along messages, because I'd kind of left everyone hanging when I went to the hospital, but it would have been great to be able to talk to them directly. And it's not just that I wanted to check in. I also wanted to ask my mother or my girlfriend to consult with some other doctors, to make sure I was getting the right treatment. But the people from the team kept telling me I was getting the best possible care, so I took them at their word. Other than that one doctor who wanted to cut me open, the folks working on me were very reassuring. They seemed to know their stuff.

Nobody could say for sure how I'd come down with these parasites, but the best guess was that it was either the street meat I'd eaten from the food cart in front of my building the day I arrived, or the cat I'd stupidly touched outside my apartment door while I was preparing food. The cat didn't seem dirty or mangy or diseased in any way, but I couldn't remember if I'd washed my hands after collecting the can of tuna or petting him before going back to the kitchen and handling pasta and veggies and whatever. After I cook pasta for myself, I have my hands in the pot, tossing all those noodles around, so this could have done it. Or maybe that street meat was tainted and hadn't been cooked properly.

Whatever it was, it nearly did me in.

—⁂—

At this point I'd missed my first team practice, and I hadn't even slept a night in my fancy apartment, so this wasn't exactly the introduction to Benghazi I'd been expecting. It wasn't any kind of introduction at all, really, but I was determined to make up for the time I'd lost. I got it in my head I wouldn't miss another practice, so I planned to drag myself to the arena the next day to meet my new teammates. I didn't want them thinking I was soft, didn't want to get off on the wrong foot with my coach. And mostly, I didn't want the Qaddafi family thinking they'd made a mistake in bringing me over.

Alexis wasn't exactly happy with this plan. We finally had a chance to talk when I got back from the hospital, and she kept telling me to come home. That had been, like, her mantra, ever since things turned to shit in Skopje: "Come home, Alex. Come home." It was her answer to everything. She even called my mother and got her working on me to come home, too. But they could see I was feeling a whole lot better than I had just a couple of hours earlier, once we started talking. They could see I was getting my strength back, so they backed off—not all the way, but enough so we agreed to disagree.

The next day, I found a way to make it to practice. I was still dragging, but once Mr. Ahmed made all the introductions and we got down to playing, it felt to me like my teammates were dragging even more. I wasn't about to push myself, but it's like I didn't have to, the way these other guys were playing. It's like they were sleepwalking through practice, like they were zombies. I couldn't understand it. Here I'd been laid up in bed for more than two days, shitting up a storm, riddled with parasites, unable to eat, and yet I was running the floor with all these professional athletes and they were the ones shuffling up and down the court.

It didn't help that our coach, Sherif Azmy, was famous for running his players into the floor. This guy was like a local legend. I'd read up on him before coming to Benghazi, read that he was from Egypt originally but had learned the ins and outs of the game from all these great coaches in the States. He had, like, a thousand different plays for a thousand different situations. Okay, so maybe that's an exaggeration, but there were, like, twenty different half-court sets, maybe a half-dozen inbound plays, maybe another half-dozen ways to beat the press. A lot of our practice time was spent going over all these different plays, and then we'd scrimmage, hard. Shoot some free throws, then scrimmage hard some more. But this was my first practice, and all I was seeing was guys who wanted to be someplace else—*anyplace* else.

We took a break after a while, and I got to talking with one of my new teammates, a six-ten center from Senegal named Moustapha Niang—a talented all-around player who could even play the wing and hit threes. He was the only other international player on the team, and we'd go on to become good, good friends. We were both outsiders looking in, so that became our common ground, and here in this first session, Moustapha filled me in on what was going on, told me our teammates were in a bad, desperate mood. He'd been in Benghazi since September, so he knew his way around. He told me the team was under tremendous pressure to win all the time, but now especially. Already they had lost three games in a row, so the players were tentative, nervous. It was only practice, but almost everyone seemed like they were afraid to make a mistake. Even in drills, even while we were scrimmaging, nobody wanted to be the one to screw things up.

Moustapha said, "If we lose another game, bad things will happen."

I said, "What bad things? You mean the coach will run us hard in practice? You mean some players might get benched?"

"No," Moustapha said. "Worse."

He did not explain further, but I learned from my new teammates that in Libya, when you played for Colonel Qaddafi's Al-Nasr team, you were expected to win. If you lost, you would carry a great shame. If you lost, you would not be paid. If you lost, you would be beaten. Qaddafi's strongmen would visit the locker room after the game and shove you against the lockers, hard. They'd hit you with sticks and clubs. Then they'd drag you into a bathroom stall and rough you up some more.

I asked Moustapha about this the next day, on our way to my first game. We were traveling to Tripoli on the team's private jet,

NBA style. Nobody issued us any airline tickets. Nobody asked us to walk through security. We just stepped on the plane, stretched out, and took off, and it was hard for me to consider the contrast between such extravagance and the brutality I was hearing about in the locker room, behind the scenes. On the one hand, they treated us like royalty, and on the other hand, like slaves.

I said, "Moustapha, is this true what I'm hearing? Qaddafi's men beat us if we don't win?"

Moustapha said, "The foreign players, me and you, we don't have to worry."

I did not take these words as reassuring. Instead, they filled me with caution and concern. I did not want to be singled out for special treatment, but at the same time I did not want to be dragged and beaten. For the first time in my life, I was scared to step onto a basketball court; for the first time, I understood what it meant to play under pressure.

Before the game, I was visited on the court by another of Qaddafi's sons—Saadi, Mutassim's older brother. Saadi Qaddafi was supposedly a great soccer player, and I guessed he was the real sportsman of the family—one of them, anyway. While his players were warming up, he came down to the floor, surrounded by eight or ten young men in military garb and another eight or ten young boys in street clothes. Saadi himself was dressed in pressed jeans and a long-sleeved, button-down shirt. He crossed the floor to where I was standing, and we shook hands.

"We have been waiting for you," he said pleasantly. "We are going to win tonight, yes? We are going to win the championship this year, yes?"

I could only agree. I was afraid to go against this man or his family. Also, I could see from the commotion in the arena that Colonel Qaddafi himself was taking his own seat in the stands, alongside military personnel. I was still talking to Saadi, but at the same time I could not keep my eyes off his father. All around the arena, the crowd seemed to take Qaddafi's appearance in stride. To these fans in Tripoli, it was no big thing for the colonel to appear at a sporting event dressed in his military whites, especially to cheer on one of *his* teams, but to me it was like playing in the Roman Colosseum before Caesar.

Saadi Qaddafi gestured towards his father and said, "My entire family, we are happy you are here."

I followed Saadi Qaddafi's gaze and met his father's eyes. The Libyan dictator seemed to flash me a little nod.

Before he prepared to take his own seat, Saadi Qaddafi had one more thing he wanted to discuss. He asked me about my religion. The question kind of threw me—the timing of it, mostly. Right there on the floor of the arena, in front of thousands of people, with the game about to begin. At first I could not think how to answer. I remembered that in northern Nigeria, when I was growing up, Muslims and Christians had been at each other's throats. Literally. I could only assume that the Qaddafi family was fully aware of my background, my beliefs. They must have known I was born and raised as a Christian, that I came from a churchgoing family. But to tell the truth was to put me in conflict with the Muslims who had brought me here to play basketball. And to tell a white lie was to let it be known that I could not be trusted.

Either way, I was screwed.

"I am a Christian man," I finally said.

There was nothing else to say. I was, after all, a young man of faith. I could not go against that faith or my church or my family, even if it was only to appease my hosts. I could only speak from my heart and tell my new employer what he already knew.

"That is no problem," Saadi Qaddafi replied beneath a wry smile. "There is only one God up there."

As I returned to my warm-up, I noticed I was shaking.

———〜〜〜———

We won that first game by about ten points, and this was significant for a number of reasons. The first and most important of these was that it changed the mood of our locker room from dark to light. Basically, it changed the team's fortunes. The whole way to Tripoli, all during the warm-up, even during our half-time talk, my new teammates had been tight and tense, like you wouldn't believe. I'd never seen anything like it on a basketball court. Basically, they'd been scared shitless, and I can't imagine how Coach Sherif or the Qaddafi family expected us to play good, winning basketball if we were scared shitless.

Most of these guys didn't speak any English, and they didn't know anything about me or my game other than the fact that I should have started out playing with them about a week earlier, when I was first signed to Al-Nasr. First there'd been the delay with my visa, then there'd been those few days in the hospital, so it must have felt to my teammates like they'd been waiting on me for the longest while. And, for the most part, it's not like any one player can turn around an entire basketball team. It's just that the whole time they were waiting, they were also losing. Not getting paid. Getting hit with sticks instead. One of my teammates actually had a black eye he'd tried to cover up with some kind of concealer. Another guy had bruises up and down his back.

It was sick. Strange and sick.

The big win was also significant because Mr. Ahmed charged into our locker room after the game and started handing out envelopes—each filled with 1,500 dinar, which at the time was comparable to about $1,000. To me, in English, he said, "Here, this is from our leader." He said the same thing to Moustapha when he handed him his envelope. To everyone else, he spoke in Arabic. The entire team got envelopes. The coaches got envelopes. Many of them had not been paid for weeks and weeks, so this was more than just a bonus. This was like a lifeline.

It's amazing the way everybody, everything, changed on the back of this one win. The whole way here, on the team jet to Tripoli, the players had been quiet and tense and serious—and now, the whole way back to Benghazi, everyone was laughing and singing and dancing in the aisles.

I sat for a while on the flight home with Sherif Azmy. I was drawn to him right away. I liked the way he coached, how he saw the game. We'd only known each other a couple of days, but I felt comfortable around him. Already I could see that he would be a good coach for me, that this team could play well for him if only we could play without being afraid to lose.

We sat quietly for a while and watched the guys on the team whoop it up and shake loose the fear and frustration of the past weeks. It was like a heavy weight had been lifted. After a while of this, Coach Sherif turned to me and said, "You will help this team, Alex. I believe this. You will change the way we play."

I said, "I only want to fit in, Coach. I want to help and fit in, that's all."

The truth about this first game was that I'd only made a small contribution. I'd played okay, but I was still weak from the parasites. Also, I was not used to my teammates. I had not yet learned many of Coach Sherif's plays. The real difference maker in this game was my friend Moustapha. He was dominant, so I could not accept all of the backslaps and congratulations from my coach and teammates. I did not deserve them, not yet.

Coach Sherif went on to tell me that the rest of the team had seen my exchange with Saadi Qaddafi before the game. They'd even seen the slight nod that may or may not have passed between me and Colonel Qaddafi. Here I'd thought this was a private, personal moment, but it had played out right there on the court, so of course everyone had seen it.

He said, "Everyone in the arena, they saw it, too. You are now an important person in this country. You have been welcomed by Colonel Qaddafi and his family. In all of Libya, people will know who you are. You will never have to buy a meal, a drink, anything. You have their blessing."

I don't know about the blessing part, but Coach Sherif was right about everything else. For the next six weeks, Al-Nasr kept winning and winning. For the next six weeks, I had the time of my basketball life—playing in front of big crowds, playing at a high level. Wherever I went in Benghazi, people greeted me warmly. They took good care of me. My teammates did, too. They connected my arrival to the turnaround of our season, and they were happy to have Qaddafi's strongmen off their backs—literally off their backs. They were happy to be getting paid—not just these occasional bonuses, but their salaries, too.

All was right in my little corner of Benghazi.

I step quietly into the hallway, careful to remain unseen, undetected. I have to keep myself from racing to Mr. Ashraf's side to see if he's okay, because I can only imagine that whoever did this to him is lying in wait to do the same to me.

My thoughts turn to Mr. Ashraf's daughter, Ariel. I wonder if she has seen her father like this. I wonder if she is safe. But I do not have to wonder for very long, because while I am peering into the hall, I hear a girl scream. It is a scream filled with pain and terror, and it seems to crawl up the stairwell to the seventh floor, surrounded by echoes. Always, the activity in the hallway is amplified. The noises from the floors below carry up the stairwell and bounce off the hard walls. The whole time I've lived here, these hallways have been filled with extra-loud noises, the sounds of my neighbors coming and going, but this morning the noises are louder still. Louder and darker and more threatening.

At first it is impossible for me to tell if these new screams are coming from around the corner of the seventh-floor hallway or from the stairwell, so I step carefully out into the scene. I quickly scan the hallway and the landing by the stairwell, but I don't see the girl. I hear her, but I don't see her. I see her fallen father out of the corner of one eye—and then, with the other eye, I see one of the rifles from before. It has been set aside on the stairwell, just a few feet away from where I am standing, skulking. It looks as if it's been kicked to this spot in haste. Then I hear grunting coming from the same direction as the girl's screams. Male grunting. I follow the sound and peer down the stairwell and see one of the two soldiers who'd pounded through my door, his uniform pants bunched down around his ankles.

The picture is confusing, but then it comes clear. I put two and two together and think I'm about to be sick. I see Ariel bent over the railing, screaming, the soldier positioned behind her, grunting. It is a terrible, terrible thing. My head fills with all kinds of rescue plans. I'm thinking about how I can save this poor girl being raped on the stairwell of her own apartment building, just a few feet away from her dying father. I do not see the second soldier, so I think I might be able to reach for the rifle. I think maybe I can hold this guy at gunpoint and get him off Ariel, and then blow him away. So this becomes my plan—to grab the AK-47 from where it has been kicked aside, but as I reach for it, I am startled by yet another series of movements from another part of the stairwell.

It is the other soldier, of course. He has not strayed far from his partner. He sees me reach for the rifle and comes charging at me, shouting furiously in Arabic. His own rifle is pointed at me as he approaches, and for a long moment I think I'm about to be shot. Right here, right now. I think it's all over for me, but he doesn't shoot. Instead he jabs at my chest with the rifle and backs me towards my apartment door, which has been flung open. He spits a bunch of commands at me as he jabs and points and pushes me along, and I can only do as he says, as I think he says. I put my hands up in the air to remind him I'm unarmed and backpedal.

I hate that I'm retreating, that I don't have it in me to help this girl, to fight, but there's nothing I can do. I'm outmanned, outflanked. But at the same time, I'm pissed. I realize, backpedaling, that these asshole soldiers can't understand me, the same way I can't understand them, so I start cursing them out like crazy. The language barrier makes me brave.

I say, "I'm gonna cut your fuckin' throat, you no-good piece of shit!"

I say, "You fuckin' coward!"

I say, "Leave her alone, assholes!"

I say all these things and more, but they don't mean a whole lot. It's something to say, that's all, and this is how I allow myself to be backed all the way into my apartment. This is how I retreat. Hands up, threatening these motherfuckers like I'm in control of the situation, when in reality I'm in control of shit. I'm completely defenseless, powerless, defeated.

The asshole, coward, piece-of-shit soldier with the rifle pulls the door closed behind me, while the other asshole, coward, piece-of-shit soldier on the stairwell continues abusing this poor girl. I can hear her wailing through the steel door, and I fall to the ground with heartbreak. Oh my God, I've got no life in me at all, and I just start crying, man. I lean my head back against the door, and for a moment I just rest it there, and then I start banging it against the door, over and over. Like I'm beating myself up for not being able to help this girl, like this is my punishment. The whole time I'm crying, louder and harder, to where it's like full-on weeping. This is probably the lowest moment of my life, I think. This is probably the beginning of the end for me.

Yes, I am safe, for now. Yes, I am protected by the fact that I'm a professional basketball player, living in Mutassim Qaddafi's apartment, for now, although in reality these things mean shit. I know this much. But I also know that whatever happens from here on in, things will get worse before they get better. Way worse.

SEVEN | BENGHAZI

(After)

HERE, AT LAST, my two stories run into each other. Here, at last, the fight for my basketball life becomes the fight for my actual life.

So there I was, holed up in my apartment, the world turning to shit outside my window, a hideous violence taking place on the other side of my front door—and me, reduced to helpless tears, not knowing what to do to set things right. It was probably the worst, most unimaginable moment of my entire life.

God, I was straight-up terrified. I don't think I ever felt so alone, so immobilized, so helpless. I thought I was about to die, and probably in a horrible way. I thought my neighbor Ariel was about to die along with her father, Mr. Ashraf, if they weren't dead already. I thought I'd never make it out of here alive, that I'd never see my parents, my siblings, Alexis again.

Like I said, I was in a bad, bad way.

It was at this point—late that first morning, into early

afternoon—that I lost all sense of time. The first couple of hours I had a clear sense of where I was, of what was going on, but then it all kind of fell away. That's when the hard-core truth of what I was seeing seemed to swallow me up. The real became surreal. The hours began to blend into each other. The days, too, before long. I believe I spent the rest of that first day just praying, to be honest with you. I must have said about thirty Our Fathers, all the way through. And each time I said it, it wasn't in a going-through-the-motions kind of way. I didn't just spit out the first line. No, I said it for real, like the words would somehow save me.

Our father, who art in heaven . . .

Time just dragged and dragged like you wouldn't believe, but then, on the other end of that, I did notice that the sun set pretty quickly. Funny, but that's what registered, from that first day. At that time of year, in that part of the world, the sun goes down around six thirty, and in my helpless stupor, it felt to me like it went down in a hurry. Like the world needed to close the curtain on this ugly, ugly scene. And it had only gotten uglier as the day went along. The noises outside my window, the gunfire, the shouting, the tanks rolling through the streets . . . I couldn't even bring myself to look, to see what was going on.

I couldn't bring myself to do much of anything.

Praying, that was about all I could handle. Praying, that was my one way to hold on to any shred of humanity after the things I'd just seen. I set it up in my head like a healing antidote. And it's not like praying didn't come naturally to me. I already prayed every day, when I got up in the morning and when I went to sleep at night. And here's the thing: I'd always been a drop-to-my-knees-by-the-side-of-the-bed type of person when it came to praying, ever since I was a little kid, only here I was basically lying on the floor or sitting by the window, so I did my praying right where I was. For a good part of that first day and probably into the second, I was hugging close to this heavy metal bookcase my landlord had positioned by one of the windows—I guess under the thinking that if a stray bullet happened to find its way into the apartment, I'd have some protection. I just sat or lay by that big old bookcase, praying.

I wasn't really thinking straight that whole first afternoon. I didn't sleep much, either, I don't think. I just kind of hugged my knees and rocked back and forth and ticked away the minutes—praying, not thinking, hoping that whatever was going on out there on the street would find a way to die down before it reached all the way up here. From time to time I'd double-back to the kitchen faucet, the bathroom faucet, just to see if the water had come back on. I'd check my laptop, my phone. I'd wonder how the hell I'd get out of there, what my next move might look like . . . if I even *had* a next move.

I was in shock, I realize now. I was grieving—for the girl on the stairwell, for her father, for the man pulled across the street by his wife and daughter. But also for the life I'd left behind back home, a life I didn't think I'd ever see again. Yeah, it had only been a couple of hours, but those hours were filled with such darkness and danger that they left me thinking I'd never get out of this sorry-ass place alive.

From time to time, I'd muster the strength or the courage or the interest to look out the window, and for a few moments I'd stare at the burning police station across the way. The building was only six or seven stories high—same as my apartment building—

but the protesters had set fire to it while people were still inside, so a lot of the folks on the upper floors had been driven to the roof, where they could breathe fresh air. These poor people were probably terrified, but they were standing on the roof directly across the plaza from my window, maybe fifty yards away. It was close enough that we could lock eyes, so we'd just stare and stare at each other. It was deeply weird, now that I think back on it, but at the time it felt like there was an important, almost intimate connection between us—between me and all these displaced, terrified police officers and support workers, looking out at each other from across the way, six or seven stories above all that deadly madness on the street.

After a couple more hours, I realized I hadn't heard another sound from my neighbors' apartment, the ones with the pass-through in my kitchen, not since first thing that morning, so I crossed to the opening and called out to them. No response. I called out again—and again there was no response. I remembered there was a brother or an uncle or a family friend who used to come by my neighbors' apartment all the time. I'd be in the hall-way talking to Miriam, or maybe we'd be visiting through the pass-through window, and I'd hear this booming, thuggish voice. His name was Amram, and his English was decent, and I thought he was a great character. Larger than life, you know. He was the type of guy who puffed out his chest and said things like "Hey, anybody bother you, I'll put a hole in their head." That type of thing. He reminded me of the trash talkers you always see on the basketball court—the ones who got game, not the ones who are just talk. He wore his hair in a slicked-back way, thought of himself as a gangster. He had a thing about Egyptians—for some

reason, he just hated Egyptians. I'd gone down to the corner market with him a couple of times, and we'd see an Egyptian crossing
the street, and he'd turn to me and say, "Fuckin' Egyptians," like
I was supposed to know what he meant.

He carried himself like someone who mattered, this guy, and
I guess the reason I thought of him that first afternoon was
because I must have assumed Miriam and her family were with
him somehow. This was a guy who could take care of himself, a
guy who was plugged in and filled up with confidence, so thinking
of him allowed me to believe my neighbors were okay.

The whole time, whenever I tuned my ears to listen, there was
the sound of gunfire rising from the streets below. Sometimes
there'd just be a single shot, every now and then. Sometimes there'd
be a whole volley. Sometimes there'd be the rapid-fire machine-
gunning I'd seen and heard from the roof, coming from the assault
rifle that had been mounted to the top of that one SUV. I was too
chickenshit to climb back upstairs to get a better look at what was
going on in the streets. I was too scared, even, to poke my head out
into the hallway.

I was in the middle of a war zone, I told myself—and this was
my bunker up here on the seventh floor, in an apartment belong-
ing to Mutassim Qaddafi. This was my foxhole. And I wasn't
moving from it anytime soon. No, sir.

There was no running water, but I had a bathroom, so at least
I wasn't living like an animal. Not yet. The only thing was, I
couldn't flush the toilet—I mean, I could flush it once, but it
wouldn't refill, so right away I started pissing in the tub. I knew
I'd run out of drinking water before long, and sure enough, that's
what happened. I took to filling a small cup with water from the

toilet and soaking a tea bag in it to fool myself into thinking it was from the tap. I told myself it was toilet tea, which made it sound just a little more appetizing, and I was pretty good about swallowing that shit down, making sure I didn't get all dehydrated. Also, I still had to take all those parasite pills, so I needed something to wash them down.

I ran out of food before too long as well, so after the first couple of days, there was nothing left to shit out of my system. If I had to go to the bathroom, I'd go in a bag and knot it up and leave it in the corner. Yeah, it was gross, but when you're in the middle of it, doing what you have to do, you don't think of it as gross. You just go about your business. You do what you have to do to survive, to get by, and then one day you look up and there are all these little plastic bags filled with shit, all lined up against the back wall of a room you don't use anymore except when you need to set down the next bag.

The only clock I knew was the sun. I didn't wear a watch. If I wanted to know the time, I'd always just looked at my cell phone or maybe the digital clock in the kitchen, but everything was out, so there was no way to tell. There was just one moment after another, one hour after another, one day after another . . . all piled up and wearing me down. Instead of time, there were these sudden markers to stamp the moment. On the third or fourth day, a building collapsed across the street. I heard this enormous boom and felt our building kind of shake. On the fourth or fifth day, I heard planes flying overhead and bombs dropping all over the city. I later learned that the Libyan military had been caught off guard by the sudden surge of protesters in the streets of Benghazi, and it took them those first few days to ramp up a response and try to take back the city.

As soon as I heard those bombs going off, I started to freak. I'd been freaking all along, but this was a whole new worry. I lived in one of the tallest buildings on the square, so I figured we were a target. I figured I was done.

My whole thing, the whole time, was that someone would come for me. That one thought kept me going—but really, it was a nonsensical thought. There was no logical reason for me to be thinking in this way. Coach Sherif had already fled the country, and the folks in the Al-Nasr office had known where I was all along and hadn't made any attempt to reach me. I don't even know if there was anything they could have done, only that Mr. Ahmed hadn't sent anyone to check on me—not that I could tell. Still, for some reason, I was still clinging to the thought that folks were looking out for me, that help was on its way. Like I said, it was nonsense. There was no reason for me to be thinking like this, but at the same time it kept me from going completely bat-shit crazy. It gave me something to believe in, something to hope for. And it kept me in place—meaning, it kept me from running wildly through the streets of Benghazi, through what was basically a war zone, and getting myself killed.

Each time the sun came up, I let my hopes rise to meet it. I brushed my teeth with toilet water, splashed some water on my face to get ready. I kept telling myself that if someone was coming for me, I wanted to look good. I wanted to be fresh. I'd take my shirt off and rub a stick of deodorant under my arms, but all I was doing was putting deodorant on top of funk. It was the illusion of hygiene, that's all, the charade of getting ready, but I talked myself into thinking I was making myself presentable.

Actually, I did a lot of talking to myself. In retrospect, I probably should have been writing stuff down, keeping some kind of journal—just as a way to keep my mind sharp and focused. But instead I was like Tom Hanks in *Cast Away*, the way I kept these running conversations going. Or sometimes I was like the doctor in that Bruce Willis movie *Tears of the Sun*. Remember that one? Bruce Willis plays a Navy SEAL type sent to Nigeria to rescue an American doctor who'd been sent on some humanitarian mission gone bad. The whole time you're watching that movie, you're thinking the United States military is about to descend on the scene and rescue this doctor, so I put myself in the same place. I got it in my head that a couple of Delta Force guys were about to burst through my heavy steel door and rescue my ass, and I kept saying as much. Out loud. I'd say, "Any minute now, Alex. They're on their way." Desperate, hopeful . . . but then something would turn in my mind and I'd go the other way entirely. I'd start saying, "Nobody's coming for you, Alex. Everyone's forgotten about you."

Still, I tried to keep to my routines. I prayed. I took my parasite medicine. I bagged my shits and drank my toilet tea. I even tried to exercise. I'd do push-ups—sets of twenty-five and thirty-five, the same way I'd been doing them since high school—but after a couple of days and then maybe a week or more of not eating and hardly drinking, I'd catch a glimpse of myself in the mirror, looking all emaciated and gaunt and wiry, and wonder what the hell I was doing. I was getting weaker by the day, to where I was just skin and bones. I took my shirt off once and stared and stared because I could see all my ribs.

Sometimes I'd look in the mirror and see myself as a kid. The first time it happened, it scared the crap out of me, but the second time I gave myself over to it. I'd see myself at three, six, nine years old and just start talking. I'd stare down my old self and have these long, specific, in-the-moment conversations with the little kid I once was. For real. I was just so completely delusional, but I talked and talked. And, I could swear it, the little me seemed to talk back. It was a two-way conversation, and when I was in the middle of one of these talks, I noticed that the face looking back at me in the mirror was always smiling. I'd see myself at twelve, at fifteen, and it struck me that I was so innocent, so happy.

It was kind of spooky, but I looked forward to these visions, these visits. I never knew when they'd come on, but I'd pass a mirror or catch my reflection in one of the windows and there I'd be—a little kid, looking back through the glass, wondering what the hell had happened to me. And then, every once in a while, I'd see high school Alex, Georgetown Alex, Alcorn State Alex, Skopje Alex . . . and he wasn't looking so innocent. He wasn't looking so happy. There was all this *stuff* now weighing on him. On me. Something had changed, and I'd say, "How can I get back to you guys?" Or "I miss you guys."

In this way, I filled my days. Time didn't fly. It didn't creep. It just came and went, came and went. I didn't sleep, though. Not in any kind of traditional way. I'd grab ten- or fifteen-minute naps here and there. Not just that first night, not just that first week, but the whole way through. All day long, all night long, I'd catch what little sleep I could just lying on the floor, leaning up against the wall, wherever I happened to be. It never even occurred to me to crawl into my bed and call it a night—I guess on the thinking that I had to stay vigilant.

Every few hours, I'd check my phone to see if I could get a call to go through. I'd dial Mr. Ahmed, Alexis, my parents . . . but when I couldn't get a signal, I'd shut the thing off to preserve the battery. Same with my laptop. I'd fire it up a couple of times a day and walk around the apartment with it looking for a Wi-Fi signal, then I'd shut it down.

In my mind, I was all about the battery—but the only batteries I was thinking of were for my phone and my computer. I wasn't thinking in terms of my own battery. I wasn't thinking of ways to keep myself charged. I was just passing the time and muddling through.

After about a week, I was down to a single stick of butter and some salt and pepper, but the fridge had been out, so the butter had most likely turned. Still, I pinched a few small bites of it every few hours, just to keep me going. I was hungry as hell. It's like I was being tortured, the way these sharp, sharp pains kept shooting through me. It tested my will, tested my heart. I found that if I lay on my back on the hard floor, it helped. For hours, I'd just lie there, staring at the ceiling, trying to suppress the hunger, and then, as soon as I moved, as soon as I sat up, the pains would come stabbing back. That's what it felt like—like I was being stabbed in the stomach, over and over.

It was excruciating. And yet, at the same time, it was also nothing. It was nothing and everything, all at once.

—⟋ɱ⟍—

One morning, about seven or eight days into my confinement, I opened my eyes from a brief catnap and noticed an unfamiliar wetness at my cheek, which had been pressed to the floor by the door to the bathroom. It was still dark, but the sky had just started to brighten, so I put the time at about six a.m. I couldn't understand the wetness at first, couldn't place it. Then, for a beat or two, I did a little jump for joy in my head, because I'd decided that the wetness meant the water had been turned back on.

It was a foolish leap of logic, I realize now, but at the time I let my head fill with an adrenaline shot of hope. I thought, *Okay, the worst of it is over.* I thought, *Here on in, I'll find my way through.* I figured it was only a matter of time before the power was restored, before the phones started working again, before I could find my way back home.

But that's not exactly how it happened. What happened, actually, was that the wetness I felt was the sewage backing up. The water came up through the toilet, and there was shit and brown water and sludge all over the bathroom. And the smell! Oh, man, was it foul. Just vile. I took one step into the bathroom, then I turned and stepped right back out. I slammed the door behind me, thinking this would help. I was barefoot, so now I was just covered in shit, and there was no way to wash it off, no way to keep the sewer water from seeping through to the next room, so I grabbed a bunch of sheets and towels and a big old comforter and just threw them all down on the floor outside the bathroom door. Then I threw some powder on that mess of linen, to kind of mask the stench.

Luckily, the sewage didn't reach all the way into the living room, so I was able to move around out there pretty much as before, but the apartment still stank something fierce. And, even worse, I was now out of water, so I went from this momentary high of thinking the water had been miraculously turned back on to realizing I'd have to do without the toilet water I'd been sipping and bathing in for the past week or so. Just like that, I went from thinking I was saved to knowing I was screwed.

For the rest of that day, I moved around in a blind funk. I listened to the shouts and the gunfire on the streets below and thought it was just like so much noise. I looked down at all the violence and the protests and the chaos and thought it was like some damn screen saver, just something going on in the background. I was numb to it . . . to *all* of it. I couldn't think what to do. But then, when I was sitting and staring out the window, daydreaming, I got an idea. I noticed three big flowerpots by the windowsill, and I guessed there'd probably be a couple of ounces of rainwater trapped in the saucers beneath the pots. Dirty, muddy, wormy rainwater—the stuff you don't even notice when your world is set right. And sure enough, there it was. I grabbed one of the flowerpots and tipped it over. Set a cup right beside it to catch the runoff. Then I took a spoon and tried to filter out the worst of the sludge and the soil, and I could almost convince myself that it wasn't nasty, that it was drinkable. And it was. Just barely.

One thing I noticed when I started digging around in those flowerpots was that they were filled with worms and bugs, so later that day, or maybe it was the next morning, I gathered up whatever will I still had and started poking around in the pots, looking for something to eat. I was absolutely starving, would have eaten just about anything, so I couldn't let myself think this was so gross or awful. It was just survival, man. That's all. That's how bad those hunger pains had gotten, after just a few days. They pushed me all the way to fishing in flowerpots for bugs and cockroaches and worms. The first time I did this, I took a cup

and pinched four or five roaches and took them back inside. Then I
sat and sat and stared at those suckers, trying to muster up the
courage to actually eat one. I'd seen a show on the Discovery
Channel, *Man vs. Wild*, in which this dude Bear Grylls would eat
rabbits and leaves and cockroaches and spiders, just to survive in
the wild. That's where I got the idea, only I couldn't bring myself to
actually do it until finally I just dropped one to the floor, stomped
on it, peeled it up off the floor and popped it in my mouth.

Oh, it was bad. Just, awful—like, a million times over. I made
a face like someone might have been looking, as if making a face
would maybe make the cockroach go down a little easier. And I
could hear the thing go all crunchy and squishy from the inside of
my mouth. But then, as soon as I swallowed, I remembered on the
show how they said you weren't supposed to crush the cockroach
before eating it. All the guts come out, so you lose all the nutri-
ents, all the protein. The key is to eat it alive, so I swallowed hard
and gave myself a sip of dirty rainwater to help wash it down
and tried to find the strength to try again. A few moments later,
I pinched another roach from the cup and popped it in my
mouth, trying superhard not to think about what I was doing.
And you have to understand, these were big-ass, African-type
cockroaches—they looked like giant water bugs—but I just
chomped down hard and bit into this sucker. This second one, the
live one, tasted kind of salty. I could feel it squirming around in
there for just a beat, and then when I bit down on it, all I could
think was that it was salty and gross.

But I kept it down. I had to fight it, but I kept it down—and I'll
be damned, I started to feel like I had a little more energy, so I ate a
couple more. Ate a couple of worms, too, so that's how I got by the

rest of the way, eating bugs and worms from the flowerpots outside my window. Switching from toilet tea to dirty rainwater tea.

Doing whatever I had to do to survive.

Meanwhile, back home, Alexis was out of her mind with worry. My mother, too. The two of them were on the phone with the American embassy, with the State Department, with representatives from the Libyan basketball federation, with anyone they could think of to hound for information. They were plugged in to the news 24-7. Soon they knew everything there was to know about the Libyan uprising, about the revolts in Tunisia and Egypt. About what the American newspapers would soon be calling the Arab Spring. Every blog post, every news report from the region just scared the crap out of them because nobody had heard from me, but they kept reading them anyway. They didn't want to miss a clue.

All they could think was the worst, right? Basically, they didn't know what to think, what not to think. If I was all right, I would have called. That's what they were afraid to tell themselves, afraid to tell each other. To say it out loud would have made it real. It would take away hope—and just then, hope was about all they had. Here's what they knew, deep down: If I was alive, I would have found a way to get a message through to someone at home, to let everyone know I was okay. So after a couple of days had passed without word from me, they thought I was dead—or at least in a really, really bad way. What else could explain my silence? Alexis went through a real depression, I found out later. After everything she'd just been through with her family, with Katrina, she now had to deal with her boyfriend's disappearance in war-torn Libya. She wouldn't get out of bed. She wouldn't eat.

But she kept working the phones, man. She was relentless. She kept searching the Internet. She was even on the phone to producers at CNN, at *Good Morning America*, trying to get them interested in my story. She was smart that way. She thought she could sell them on some local angle to this big, developing story, and then they'd have all these different reporters in the region to help track me down.

Mainly she was calling everyone she could. She even called Moustapha Niang, I learned later, because I'd used his phone when my battery ran out one night and she'd saved the number, but he couldn't tell her anything since he hadn't heard from me, either. And the whole time she and my mother kept in constant contact, comparing notes, commiserating, trying to figure their own next moves.

My agent was also doing what he could to find me. He had a whole mess of contacts in the region, so he spent some time every day trying to learn what he could. He sent me a ton of e-mails, which were all piled up and waiting for me when Internet service was finally restored a couple of weeks after the first days of the revolt: *If you get this, please call . . . . Alex, where are you?* . . . and on and on.

I knew as much, I guess. I tried not to think about it, but I knew my family was half a world away, worried sick about me. I knew my brand-new girlfriend was probably distraught. But what I didn't know, what I only learned later, was that my father was also struggling with some health issues that had nothing to do with my situation in Benghazi. He'd had a bout with prostate cancer back in 2000. In 2007, he got testicular cancer. And in 2010, about six months before I left for Macedonia, he was diagnosed with multiple myeloma, a cancer of the plasma cells. All of this I already knew, but while I was away, they'd had to pump him up with so much chemo that it might have contributed to the onset of type 2 diabetes. Either way, it wasn't good. He was really hurting, man—and my disappearance certainly wasn't helping.

I didn't even know the full extent of his type 2 diabetes, and already I was thinking not knowing what was going on with me would just about kill him. The same way it was just about killing me, not knowing what was going on with *him*. The truth was, he hadn't been doing all that well when I left for Macedonia, but my thinking at the time was that the world was smaller than it had ever been. I told myself we could talk all the time while I was away, we could visit on Skype, same as if I'd been down in Atlanta with Alexis while my folks were up in Boston. A couple of hundred miles away or a couple of thousand miles away, it didn't make much difference. Plus, if I needed to—if any kind of worst-case scenario presented itself—I figured I could always grab the next flight home.

My dad wasn't the type of person to ask me to stick around just because he was sick. He wouldn't have wanted me or any of my siblings to live our lives any differently in order to see him through his struggles. He just wanted us to live our lives. For him, that was always the bottom line—for his kids to do right by their dreams. Still, back in December, when I decided to bounce from Skopje to Benghazi, I'd called to get his take. I knew what he'd say about me going, but at the same time, I wanted to see how he felt about it, me being so far away while his health was declining. I put it out there that I didn't have to travel all the way to the

Middle East just to play basketball. I told him I could find a place
to play in the States, so I could be around if he needed me, but he
wasn't having any of that. He just said, "If it's good for you, it's
good for me." That was the same thing he always said to us whenever we were trying things out. College, graduate school, work,
relationships—if we came to him with some dilemma or other,
some move we were weighing, he'd tell us to follow our hearts,
that's all.

If it's good for you, it's good for me.

But I couldn't know any of this while I was holed up in my
apartment in Benghazi that first week. All I could do was close
my eyes and hear my father's voice, my mother's voice. I could talk
to my little-kid self in the mirror. I could picture Alexis and hope
she was doing okay—and pray that everyone I loved back home
had found a way to keep me alive in their minds, because I got it
in my head that if I was dead to them, I was dead to myself. I
mean, I was eating cockroaches, man. I was drinking mud water.
Lying about in a shit-filled apartment, afraid to open the door and
peek outside, even just to check things out.

All along, I'd tried to keep a little hope going in my own mind.
I kept thinking someone from the team would be by for me, but
with each passing day, this seemed less and less likely, and as I
moved from hopeful to hopeless, I started to think through what
needed to happen to change my situation. I was trapped in this
terrible stalemate, seven stories above an ongoing, unthinkable
battle, with absolutely no idea what to do about it. Like I said,
about the only thing I could do was pray, so I went at it, hard. For
a week, ten days, twelve, I'd been praying. All day, every day. And

now I prayed some more, only now I was praying for a miracle.

And, eventually, that's just what I got—an honest-to-God miracle.

My cell phone rang.

Twelve days in, it just started ringing. I had no idea what it was, where it was coming from, but I figured it out soon enough. I'd tucked my phone into a small travel bag I'd packed full of stuff I'd need if I had to make a quick exit—my passport, my player ID card, some money, my laptop, my phone—and left by the front door. I was still in the habit of checking my cell signal, hoping to get a call to go through, but I suppose I was checking with a little less frequency as time dragged on. I mean, that's like a classic sign of insanity, right? To keep doing the same thing, going through the same motions, over and over, and each time hoping for a different outcome. But I was stupidly hopeful, so I kept at it. Maybe I was down to a couple of times a day instead of every couple of hours, but I kept at it, and each time I was careful to kill the power to preserve the battery. At least, I meant to be careful, because I must have left it on the very last time I'd checked. That's the only thing I can think of to explain this sudden ringing from out of nowhere—but it struck me just then like a genuine miracle. Like God himself reaching down from the heavens to check in with me.

I fumbled over and dug the phone out of my bag. It was an old-school Nokia flip phone, and as I flipped it open, I saw that it was still fully charged, so I knew I hadn't left it on for long.

It was my teammate, Moustapha, calling from the other side
of the city. I think I answered it on the fourth or fifth ring—
that's how long it took me to process what was happening
and to muster the strength to "race" to the front door. It's a
good thing it didn't go to voice mail, because I might never have
gotten another signal.

He said, "My brother, how you doin'?"

I said, "Moustapha, good to hear your voice. I'm not doin' too
good, man."

He filled me in on what was going on with him. I filled him
in on what was going on with me. He was all the way on the
other side of the city, maybe three or four miles from me, and
where he was it wasn't like the middle of a war zone. He had
running water. He had electricity, although his power had been
going in and out. He had an occasional cell signal, and he'd
been trying to get me on the phone for the past two weeks. He
hadn't left his apartment, either, but he'd been in touch with the
outside world. He had food. Compared to me, he was styling.

He said, "You talk to Mr. Ahmed?"

I said, "No, man. I haven't talked to anyone. My phone's been
out the whole time."

He said, "Then it must be that you haven't spoken to your family, to your girlfriend?" He was asking, but he knew the answer.

I said, "Nobody."

He said, "Your girlfriend, she called me. She is worried
about you."

This was the first I'd heard that Alexis had been calling all
over Libya. It made no sense to me at first, but Moustapha
explained how she had gotten his number, told me how frantic

she'd been on her end, so I made him promise to call her back for me. Call, text, whatever. Just find a way to let her know I was okay, tell her I loved her.

I said, "Just in case I can't get a signal. Just in case this one call from you is all there is."

We made plans to talk again the next day at the same time. Moustapha's power was out at the time, so he was worried about draining his battery—and, frankly, I was still a little shocked the call had come through at all. I was scared to end the call, though, because Moustapha had just appeared out of nowhere, like a lifeline. Like a breath of fresh air. If I let him go, I might never get him back. I thought he might end up being the last person I'd ever speak to—that's how desperate and up against it I was feeling.

As soon as we hung up with each other, I frantically dialed Alexis in the States, but I kept getting the same "call failed" messages I'd been seeing all along.

I tried redialing Moustapha's line, but the same thing happened. Each time, the same thing happened.

Finally, I shut the phone off and put it back in my bag.

The next day, at about the same time, I switched it back on and waited like a crazy person for Moustapha to call. I sat with my back to the front door, the phone in my hand. It started ringing soon enough—a whole other miracle on the back of that first one.

He started out the same way he had the day before. "My brother," he said, "how you doin', man?"

I said, "Still not good, man."

He told me he'd gotten through to Mr. Ahmed. He said, "He thinks he can get us out of here. He wants us to meet him in his office."

I thought, *How the hell is that supposed to happen?* I said, "I can't leave here, man. I don't know how it is over by you, but it's bad over here. I'm afraid to even step into the hallway."

Moustapha was patient, encouraging. I think he knew he had to push me, but he didn't want it to come across like he was pushing me. He reminded me that he hadn't been outside his apartment yet, either. He said we needed to find a way to get to Mr. Ahmed's office, or else there was no telling how long we would be trapped inside our apartments. He said, "Either we will make it or we will not. Do you think you can try?"

I said, "Maybe." That's all I said at first. *Maybe.* Like I didn't even know if I could find the courage to leave my apartment.

But of course I had to try. There were people waiting on me back home. There was the whole rest of my life waiting on me back home. There were all those younger Alexes waiting on me, too, on the other side of the mirror. So before signing off with Moustapha, I said, "I will see you or I won't. I will make it or I won't."

In addition to his duties as team president, Mr. Ahmed worked as a travel agent. He kept his travel agency office in a building a few blocks away from the team offices—a little bit closer to where I lived. Even so, I had to travel through the worst of the war zone to get to him, and from the pictures I'd kept in my head from that first morning on the roof, surveying the scene, I could think of no good way for me to get from here to there.

I grabbed a hooded sweatshirt from a pile of clothes on the

floor, a pair of sweatpants, a pair of sneakers. I also grabbed the travel bag I'd packed and left by the front door. And then—slowly, tentatively—I opened the door and stepped out into the hallway. There was no one around that I could see. No sign of my neighbor, Mr. Ashref. No sign of his daughter, Ariel. No sign of the brutality that had driven me back into my apartment in the first place. No sign of the shit I was now in—just a deserted stairway landing, that's all.

I thought I'd bound down those stairs like there was a gun to my head, but I wasn't moving so well. It took moving like this for me to even notice. I was so weak from not eating, from hardly drinking, from lying around on the hard floor for two weeks, and my knees and ankles were all shot and sore. I was like an old man trying to get down those stairs. I had to hold on to the railing the whole way down. For seven flights, I clutched that railing like my life depended on it. I was hurting so bad, moving so slowly, that it took me almost ten minutes to get down those stairs, and the whole way down I kept a little conversation going in my head. I kept telling myself things like "You're halfway there, Alex. There's no going back." And "Come on, man. Don't give up now." Whatever I could think of to keep moving.

As soon as I got to the ground floor, I kind of eased over to the front door of the building and took a look around. There, on the street right outside my building, was that same group of kids I used to see on my way home from the arena, from the practice facility. The same group of mini mercenaries I'd seen on the first day of the fighting, from the roof. The soccer-mad, hoops-mad kids who greeted me like LeBron James, like Michael Jordan. Once again, from the looks of them, I guessed they were eight or

ten or twelve years old. There were five or six of them, most of
them carrying AK-47s that looked to be about half their size. They
made a damn strange picture, I'll say that. The others were carrying machetes or smaller weapons I couldn't quite make out.
They wore bandannas around their heads, some of them. They
were smoking, some of them.

They were just sitting there, hanging, loafing, guarding
the street like tiny little terrorists. I had no idea which side of
this fight they were on, but there they were, right in front
of me, and I decided my only move was to reach out to them.
My only hope was that they would be on my side for the next
little while.

I called to them from the doorway. I said, "Pssst." Just to get
their attention, you know. *Pssst.* Like we were in the movies.

They remembered me, these kids. Deep down, I knew they
would. I wasn't thinking all that clearly, but I knew to trust what
came from deep down. These kids had always greeted me as if
I was their favorite player from the Al-Nasr football club—a
Nigerian soccer player named Okocha. They thought we looked
alike. They knew I was Nigerian, same as him. They thought we
should be brothers, so they called me by his name. This was their
little joke.

One of them—the leader, I hoped—looked at me and smiled.
His face went from hard to soft in the time it took to turn his
head. He said, "Okocha!" Like he was glad to see me.

The others turned to look at me as well, and they joined in
the greeting.

"Okocha!"

As they moved towards me, I began to feel weak. That climb

down the stairs had taken the last of my energy, and I felt my legs give beneath me. One of these kids saw me start to buckle, and he reached for me, tried to hold me up. He helped me position myself against the wall, so I wouldn't fall on my face.

They were excited to see me, these kids. That's how I read the scene. They started speaking, all at once. In Arabic. I couldn't understand a word they were saying, other than the Nigerian name they had given me, so I reached into my pocket for Mr. Ahmed's card, which I handed over to the first kid. I pointed to the address. I said, "Mr. Ahmed. Mr. Ahmed."

He took the card, passed it around to his friends, then handed it back to me, and through a series of hand gestures, I was able to get them to understand that I needed them to take me to the address on the card. I can't be sure, but I think I made one of those fingers-do-the-walking motions, from those old Yellow Pages commercials, to show that I wanted to go to the address on the card.

In a flash, these kids reminded me of that group of jackals I'd encountered that one night in Macedonia, only those kids had been out to hurt me. These kids seemed to want to help. Either way, I was at their mercy. Hurt me or help me, they would decide my fate. They would take me to Mr. Ahmed's office or they would not.

One of them seemed to understand my request better than the others, so he took the lead. He stepped out in front and motioned for me to join him. He said, "Okocha, go!" He meant for me to come, to follow, so I did.

Two other kids took me by the arms, one on each side, because I was just tripping everywhere. I couldn't keep up, couldn't keep my balance.

They took me every which way. I had a vague idea of which direction we should be headed, but we were zigging and zagging, ducking into side streets and back alleys and going the long way around. And we were moving! At times they broke into a run, and the two kids on my arms were almost dragging me along, like a pull toy. My feet could hardly move fast enough to keep up. I had no idea where they were taking me. At first I thought they were just keeping to the back roads to avoid being detected, but then I started to think, *Oh, man, these kids are about to kill me. They'll drag me to some deserted alley and start hacking me to death with their machetes.*

Every once in a while the kid out in front would shout out a word I couldn't understand, and everyone would just stop and look around. Then he'd shout out something else and we'd start moving again. For ten minutes, we moved about the city in this way, beneath the sounds of gunfire and shouting and mayhem. And then we kept going for another ten minutes more, at least.

Finally we got to the address on Mr. Ahmed's card, and he came out to greet us. Before talking to me, he talked to my mercenaries. Again, I had no idea what they were saying. It seemed like the kids wanted to wait for me, and he seemed to be telling them this wasn't necessary. But, of course, they waited. They'd come all this way, so what the hell else were they going to do?

Once Mr. Ahmed was satisfied that this gang of boys meant him no harm, he turned to me. He looked me over like he was setting eyes on a long-lost relative. He said, "My boy, what has happened to you?"

I said, "What do you mean? What has happened to me has happened to everyone. We are under attack."

He said, "Yes, I suppose we are. But you are so skinny! Have you not been eating?"

A part of me was pissed to have to answer such a stupid question, but then I realized Mr. Ahmed might not have known how bad things were in my part of the city. We stood only a mile or so away from my building, but already, on the round-about way over here, I could tell that the scene on these streets was not at all like the scene on the streets of my neighborhood. I thought of it like a video game, realized it's like we'd moved from the kill zone to the perimeter. I said, "I have no food. So, no, I have not been eating. For almost two weeks, I have not been eating."

Mr. Ahmed's apartment was only two blocks from his office, so he'd been walking to work every couple of days, just to check in. It wasn't exactly business as usual, but this was his new normal since everything had turned to shit outside my apartment window. No, he hadn't been in the same kind of danger—he hadn't been gripped by the same kind of fear, at least. Maybe things were pretty much the same where he was and he was just used to it, being from this part of the world. Maybe this was how things were around here. But he'd had food. He'd been able to put his son to bed each night. He'd been able to move about without too much worry.

Me, I'd been the poster boy for too much worry. And now, standing alongside this man who worked for the Qaddafi family— a successful Benghazi businessman—I felt suddenly protected. This was probably an unreasonable thing to feel, because the rebels in the street were protesting the Qaddafi regime—that's what this whole uprising was about in the first place—but I didn't think too long or too hard about any of that stuff. I was just glad to be in this man's office.

It was March 1, 2011, a Tuesday, and for the first time in two weeks, I let myself think I was going home. All this time I'd been hoping against hope, talking myself into the thought that I would be okay, but I didn't really *know* it until just this moment.

Moustapha burst in a short while later and collected me in the biggest, longest, hardest hug I'd ever known. Oh, man, I was so, so happy to see him! I can't be sure, but I think I started to cry. Moustapha, too. It was such a joyous, emotional reunion— only once we stepped back from our hug, he started looking at me funny. Like he was checking me out. And as he did, I realized how I must have looked to him, to Mr. Ahmed . . . to this band of boys probably still waiting for me on the street outside Mr. Ahmed's office. I'd stared at myself in the mirror a whole bunch of times when I was trapped in my apartment, but I'd never really considered the changes in my appearance. One day to the next, I looked pretty much the same. But now, through Moustapha's eyes, I saw what he saw. My teeth had turned yellow. I'd grown a wisp of mustache and beard—these long wiry hairs just kind of bursting from the sides of my face, from my chin. I'd lost about twenty pounds. My eyes were all hollow and dull, and I'd developed these weird black spots underneath them—they're still there, as I write this. My hair was all messed up and dirty, and I'm sure I smelled like complete crap.

Moustapha looked me up and down. It felt like I was on display, but he told me later he was trying to figure out what had happened to me, that's all. When I got to Libya just a month or so earlier, I'd been big and muscular and full of energy. And now I was bent over and frail and gaunt and barely able to stand on my own. Moustapha took one good look at me and his face seemed to fill with concern, but before we could start talking and comparing notes, Mr. Ahmed came over with a tray filled with cakes and cookies and bottles of water, and I just started stuffing my face. It's like I was inhaling all this stuff, that's how hungry I was, and after a couple of fistfuls I could see myself in one of the mirrors in Mr. Ahmed's office with cake crumbs dangling all over my beard, but I didn't really care. I noticed, but I didn't really care. I was just so happy to have something to eat, something to drink.

Mr. Ahmed said we could wait out the uprising in Benghazi until we could move about freely, or he could hire a driver to take us out of the country, into Egypt. It would be about a seven-hour drive to the border, he said, and this seemed like a good plan.

But Moustapha wanted to stay. He wanted to wait for the revolution to die down. He said, "Man, they might kill us along the road."

I said, "Yes, but they might kill us here in Benghazi, too. I would rather die trying to escape than die waiting."

We never really discussed it, but Moustapha and I both knew we were in this thing together, from here on in. I wanted what he wanted. He wanted what I wanted. Where he would go, I would go. Where I would go, he would go. We just had to agree on a next move, and Mr. Ahmed didn't exactly solve our stalemate when he told us a story about a soccer player from Cameroon who'd been in the same situation just a few days earlier. Mr. Ahmed had hired a driver to take the soccer player to Egypt, but when they were stopped at a checkpoint before leaving Libya, the dude panicked and tried to make a run for it across the desert.

"The rebels, they gunned him down," Mr. Ahmed said, like the soccer player from Cameroon had it coming to him.

I didn't know what to make of this story except to think that Mr. Ahmed was telling us to keep our heads when we got to a checkpoint, but Moustapha heard it and started to freak. Seriously, he whipped himself into a kind of panic attack. He said, "We're gonna die here, man. We're gonna die here." Over and over, he said this.

I tried to calm him down, to get him to see the reason in Mr. Ahmed's escape plan. I wanted him to focus on the positive. I said, "If we leave, we're gonna make it. We'll be in control. If we stay here, we're done."

It was like a battle of wills, between the two of us. Moustapha wanted to stay. I wanted to go. It would come down to which one of us was stronger in his position, which one of us could convince the other.

Finally, I just started yelling at Moustapha. I said, "Listen, you got family back home waiting on you."

This seemed to turn him around, and eventually it was decided that Mr. Ahmed would arrange for a car and driver and we would leave later that night. Moustapha needed to double-back to his apartment to get his passport and a few other essential items. Me, I was feeling brave and strong and jacked up on all that cake and water, so I wanted to go back to my apartment to grab a few things, too. Mostly, I thought of those kids outside Mr. Ahmed's office with their rifles and their machetes and decided we needed some way to protect ourselves. We needed some way to fight back if we were at a checkpoint and things went bad.

I turned to Moustapha and said, "We need weapons, man."

He said, "You have a gun?"

I said, "No, but we need something in case somebody runs up on us."

Basically, I decided to go back to my apartment for the set of killer knives Mutassim Qaddafi had in his kitchen. Those would offer some protection, and I'd been thinking about them all afternoon, since heading out with my rebel escort. So we parted company at Mr. Ahmed's office and made plans to meet up later. We couldn't count on our phones to work, so we were very specific. The driver would collect Moustapha at his apartment and then come around to collect me. An hour or so after dark, I was to stand by my window and look for the car in front of a small market on the corner of my street, where I used to buy toothpaste and soap.

You know, I'm ashamed to admit it, but in the short time I was in Mr. Ahmed's office, it never once occurred to me to try my phone, to put a call through to Alexis or to my parents. I didn't ask if he had Wi-Fi, either, to see if I could send some kind of message home. I'd been so caught up in making these hasty plans for our escape that I let the moment pass, and I let the folks who loved me go on not knowing what the hell had happened to me for just a little while longer. It wasn't until I was heading out the door to make the trek back to my apartment that I even thought of checking in back home, but I guess my head was someplace else.

I fully expected those mercenary kids to be waiting for me outside on the street—and sure enough, they were right where I had left them. Mr. Ahmed explained to them that I wanted to go back to my apartment and asked them to take me there, so off we went. The return route was just as winding and haphazard as it had been on the way over, but at this point I trusted these kids to keep me safe. They knew these streets, knew what they were doing. Also, I had a lot more energy for this return trip, was able to move about on my own steam, so we made much better time. This time, when we broke into a run, I was able to keep up.

Back in my apartment, I grabbed some more clothes. I filled a small duffel and a small suitcase with crap I thought I might need, then went into the kitchen and started sorting through all those knives. I found some tape in one of the drawers, stripped to my shorts, and strapped a couple of knives to each shin. Then I put on a pair of sweatpants baggy enough to conceal them—or so I hoped.

The sun was still up when I was ready to go, so I stood by the window and waited. And waited. For a couple of hours, I waited. I tried my phone but couldn't get a signal, so I stood watch. Finally, at about eleven o'clock, I saw a car pull up in front of the market on the corner. I saw Moustapha's head in the backseat. I saw him open his window a crack and stick his hand in the air in a kind of wave, knowing I'd be looking down on him from my apartment. So I grabbed my things and raced back down those seven flights of stairs in no time flat. Earlier that day, it had taken me about ten minutes to struggle down those stairs, but this time I think I made it in just a minute or so. This time I was feeling juiced and jazzed and good to go. This time I had someplace I needed to be.

My little rebels were waiting for me by the front door to my building. I thought, *Damn, don't these kids ever go to sleep? Don't they have someplace to go?* But there they were, like they were guarding the place.

I dropped my bags and walked over to them, gave them each a hug. One by one, I told them to be safe, to be smart. I knew they couldn't understand me, but I hoped they'd take my meaning just from my tone. I hoped they could see that I cared. And I did, man. I did. They were jumping up and down, saying "Okocha! Okocha!" Smiling, dancing, waving.

—⟋m⟋—

The car Mr. Ahmed had arranged for us was really, really small. The way Moustapha was jammed into the front seat, his knees all the way up to his chest, it was like a clown car at the circus. There was hardly any room for me in the back with our few bags, but we fit ourselves in and motioned for the driver to take off. The driver didn't speak a lick of English, and I wondered what he knew of our situation. I decided I didn't care what he knew or what he understood, and I spoke to Moustapha as if we were the only ones in the car.

I handed Moustapha a couple of knives and the roll of tape and said, "Here, tape these around your legs."

Moustapha looked at the knives, and then he looked back at me. He said, "Are we really going to need these, do you think?"

I said, "How the hell do I know, man? But it's better to be prepared."

Fifteen minutes later, we were at our first checkpoint. It wasn't really a legitimate checkpoint, just a barricade in the middle of the road on the outskirts of Benghazi manned by five or six rebels with machine guns. That's what we'd taken to calling these guys patrolling the streets, *rebels*, but they were just local people—the same people I'd seen around when I first hit town. Just regular Libyan folks, you know. They wore plain old street clothes, but they moved around like they owned the place.

Our driver rolled to a stop, and the rebels started banging on the hood of the car very aggressively. We were the only car on the road. It was late, almost midnight. There was nothing else going on. I don't think I saw anyone else beyond this checkpoint. But here were these five or six guys, dressed in dark street clothes, all lined up, banging on the hood, yelling. And not just yelling but signaling—like, furiously. In Libya, the people tend to talk with their hands. When they get excited, their hands flap about their heads like they're brushing away gnats, and these guys were just flapping around like crazy, talking some big line of shit Moustapha and I couldn't understand. One of them was barking at our driver, who indicated to us that we needed to show our identification, so we handed over our passports, our player IDs.

The rebels passed our papers back and forth, started talking louder and louder, waving their hands more and more frantically. The only words we could make out were *Nigeria* and *Senegal*. They'd talk and talk, and then they'd say where we were from, and we could not imagine if this was a good thing or a bad thing. Our driver was calm, but Moustapha was starting to fidget in the front seat. This was taking way too long, and I could see that Moustapha was trying to sit on his hands, to keep himself calm. He was nervous, antsy. He kept talking to me the whole time, kind of like he was mumbling under his breath, in a voice so low no one outside the car could hear. I can't imagine that they spoke English, but Moustapha didn't even want them to know he was talking, so he whisper-mumbled. He'd say, "What's going on, Alex?" He'd say, "Man, this is not good." He'd say, "They're gonna kill us!"

I tried to talk him down from his worries, but Moustapha was whipping himself into an agitated state. He was supernervous, supertense, and at one point one of the rebels noticed this and must have thought Moustapha was reaching for something under the seat, maybe making some kind of move, so he barked out a whole other mess of words we couldn't understand, and the next thing we knew a couple of guards threw Moustapha's door open and started yanking him out of the car by the shirt. Two of the rebels had their guns drawn on Moustapha, and another one had him by the shirt, and Moustapha just kind of leaned and fell out of the low-hanging seat and onto the dirt road.

Another guy came to my door and *tap-tap-tapped* on the window, like he was telling me I was supposed to come out, too. So I did. Then he touched the roof of the car a couple of times, like he wanted me to put my hands there, so I did that, too.

The whole time, our driver seemed to be trying to calm the guards checking our papers, telling them we were basketball players, only basketball players, telling them we were just trying to get out of the country and get back home to our families. At least that's what I hoped he was saying. There was no way to know, but he'd been hired by Mr. Ahmed to deliver us safely to the border, so I assumed he had our backs. I *hoped* he had our backs.

Moustapha, though, was all jumpy, all panicky. The rebels had pulled him about twenty feet away from the car, away from me, so I couldn't tell him to just chill. One of the guards started searching me, and I wasn't nervous about him finding the knives strapped to my shins, because I wasn't really thinking about the knives strapped to my shins. I'd kind of forgotten about them—it had slipped right out of my head—but this guy didn't do such a good job patting me down, so it didn't matter. He never discovered them.

Another guard started emptying our bags out of the trunk, just dropping them in the dirt and tearing into them, but from the way these rebels were going about their business, from the way they were frisking me, I got the sense that they were a bunch of amateurs. I was still a little bit scared. I would have preferred it if they had just waved us past. But I wasn't too worried.

At this point, I turned to where Moustapha had been taken and saw one of the guards kick him in the back of the knee, which dropped my friend to the ground, and as he lay in the dirt, I locked eyes with Moustapha, and he flashed me this look that seemed to say, *Hey, we're gonna die here, man.* It was dark, but the space between us was lit by the headlights of our car, and I could almost read Moustapha's thoughts, just by his expression, and I went from not being too worried to being dead certain we were about to be killed in, like, a heartbeat. I mean, that's an aggressive, sudden move for this guy to kick Moustapha in the back of the knee like that. And it broke me, man. It left me thinking, *Shit, they're about to execute my friend, right there in the dirt, and then after that they'll come gunning for me.*

I started praying. In my head, I was praying hard. I said, *Please get us out of here, please get us out of here.* Over and over, almost like a mantra. But then suddenly, I remembered those knives taped beneath my sweatpants, and as the guy at my back stepped away from me to join his buddy rummaging through our gear, I thought, *Aw, fuck it. I will not be broken. I'm not going out like this. Better to go out fighting than to wait for these assholes to take me out.*

Before I could make a fool move, though—just as I started to reach for the knife strapped to my right leg, just as I started to imagine breaking towards the guy standing over Moustapha and stabbing him in the chest repeatedly—there was another volley of yelling in Arabic, another commotion on my side of the car. I'd been bent forward, but now I shot straight up, and as I did, the first guy was back on me, slapping my arms onto the hood of the car, and two other guys were back on Moustapha, lifting him from the dirt and dragging him to the car.

One minute Moustapha was a dead man. The next he was about to be set free. Just like that.

To this day, I've got no idea what turned these rebels around. I don't know if it was something our driver said, or if they maybe checked our player cards and decided they were messing with the wrong dudes, realized we were traveling beneath some kind of protection from the Qaddafi family. Or maybe they just got bored, decided to move on to something else. Whatever it was, they were done with us. They pounded their fists on our car a few more times to let us know they were in charge, barked out a few orders to our driver, and waved us away, like we'd been nothing but a giant nuisance.

Our shit was still scattered by the side of the road, so Moustapha and I had to spend a few long moments gathering our clothes, our laptops, our gear back into our bags. This wasn't so easy, because it was dark. The only lights were coming from our own car, but the headlights were pointing in the opposite direction of our mess, so we couldn't really see what we were doing. I'm pretty sure we ended up leaving a bunch of stuff behind, but we threw together what we could and jumped back in the car as quickly as possible before the rebels changed their minds.

A couple of hundred yards down the road, Moustapha turned towards the backseat and said, "I cannot do this again, Alex."

I said, "Don't worry, Moustapha. We're okay. We'll be okay."

He said, "They were going to kill me."

I said, "Nobody is going to kill you. We will be okay. You'll see."

I didn't believe this, but I was trying to stay positive—for Moustapha, and also for myself.

EIGHT | SALLUM

MR. AHMED HAD SAID THE DRIVE TO EGYPT should take about seven hours, but it ended up taking almost twelve. We had to stop at another four or five checkpoints along the way, and even though none of the others matched the first one in terms of life-and-death drama, they each took some time. There was always some hassle or other, some sweating it out. And after Benghazi, I should probably point out, these were all official checkpoints, with proper gates and uniformed guards. Our hearts skipped a couple of beats at every damn one of them, but we were never in the kind of danger we'd been in at that first stop, fifteen minutes into our escape.

Every gate and checkpoint we cleared, it felt more and more like we were headed home.

Finally, at about noon the following morning, we reached an enormous gate directly across from Sallum, a small Egyptian town on the Libyan border, by the Mediterranean Sea. I'd never heard of Sallum, had no idea where we were on the map—which, it turned out, was the extreme northeast corner of Libya. The United Nations had set up a kind of refugee camp there, to help process the hundreds and hundreds of multinationals who'd been trying to get out of Libya since the fighting had started a couple of weeks earlier, and almost as soon as we were sent past the final checkpoint, a volunteer worker approached our vehicle with three-packs of orange soda and a few sleeves of crackers.

We thought, *Yeah, man! Snacks!* And just on the back of this one simple kindness, we decided this place was the greatest outpost in all the Middle East, as if we'd been delivered to some kind of promised land.

But then we had to clear a few more hurdles, and soon what looked promising on the outside looked depressing on the way in. The deeper we got into the camp, the more we realized it wasn't any kind of promised land after all, wasn't any kind of oasis. It was just a way station, a limbo. No, nobody was trying to kill us, but we couldn't always tell if people were actually trying to help us, either. And the place, up close, was kind of depressing. There was trash everywhere. Hundreds and hundreds of people— thousands, maybe—were squeezed into a too-small space, being made to wait out an uncertain situation for an uncertain period of time. It was hectic, crazy. Nobody seemed to know what the hell was going on. Everywhere we looked, we saw people crying, people trying desperately to get the attention of someone in charge, children looking around frantically for their parents . . . really, it was a troubling scene.

Our driver took us to the customs area, beyond which we had to go the rest of the way on foot, so we got out of the car and collected our gear. We'd grown fond of the driver over the past dozen hours, so we hugged in parting. We kind of fumbled for a way to communicate with him, a gesture to show our gratitude. I reached in my pocket and pulled out about $300 to give to him, maybe half of what I had. I was sure Mr. Ahmed had paid him—and probably well—but I was so grateful that this man had delivered us safely to Egypt and talked us through all those checkpoints that I wanted to show my appreciation. Moustapha gave him some money, too, and we said our good-byes and followed the signs to a small building where we were supposed to have our paperwork processed.

For a half hour or so, I could look back and see our driver hanging by the main entrance, making sure we were allowed through the gate, and I remember thinking this was so above-and-beyond decent of him. The whole way here, twelve hours on crappy back roads, through the middle of the night, past sketchy checkpoints where it sometimes seemed we were about to be killed, we didn't say a word to each other, didn't even ask each other's names—and yet we were in each other's care.

Eventually, we presented our papers to a clerk seated in a booth, like you'd see at the customs counter at a small international airport. When my turn came, the clerk asked my nationality, so I said that I was both Nigerian and American. I carried two passports, and I presented them both, and I was sent to another line on the left.

When Moustapha's turn came, he told the clerk he was from Senegal, and he presented his passport and was sent to another line on the right.

Most of the people passing through were Egyptians, and they presented their passports and were sent off in a whole other direction, from where they seemed to pass through the camp fairly quickly. The Egyptians were the VIPs of this refugee camp. The Nigerians, with whom I had been huddled, and the Senegalese, with whom Moustapha had been placed, seemed to be bunched up in a kind of indefinite holding pattern, along with folks from Ghana, some Ethiopians, some Tunisians.

We weren't going anywhere just yet.

It was frustrating, maddening, but we had nothing to complain about, really. The conditions were far better here than we had any right to expect—far better than I'd imagined when I was imprisoned in my apartment or threatened at gunpoint at that first checkpoint—so for the first while I didn't even notice or think to bitch and moan. We were corralled into one giant room about the size of half a football field, separated into small groups based on our nationality. Moustapha was all the way on the other side of the room, but we were the two tallest people in there, so we were able to see each other over the crowd. We could kind of keep tabs on each other.

Underneath this one giant room, I was told, there was a giant prison barracks—which was what the place was originally designed for, I guess. This whole refugee camp was a kind of makeshift setup, thrown together at this border detention facility when things started to go bad in Libya, so the volunteers and officials were still getting their acts together, still figuring things out. Nobody had been expecting such a mass exodus of people, I don't think, and yet here we were, desperate, tired, and hungry, waiting to be sent on our way.

And the people kept coming.

After a while, I was led to another booth, where I had to present my paperwork all over again. This time the clerk said someone from my consulate would come for me in a couple of hours. Moustapha, as far as I knew, was told the same thing, so we each retreated to our separate sides of the great room and waited. I didn't mind the waiting so much. I took the time to wander around, to see what I could see, and after a while, I noticed I was in some sort of infirmary area, where I also noticed a United Nations volunteer talking on a cell phone. I hung back for a bit while he finished his call, then I asked if I could borrow his phone, maybe make a call to the States—and to my great and happy surprise, he handed it over.

One thing it helps to know: In Libya and Egypt, as it does all over that region, cell phone service works on a system of credits. There's no such thing as unlimited use—at least there's nothing for people of average means. You buy a certain number of credits, which you then use as you go, so I was careful not to take up too much of this guy's time. I figured I could make one quick call to Alexis, just to let her know I was okay, so I dialed her number, and when I heard her voice I all but melted onto the floor.

I said, "I'm in Egypt, I'm on my way home. I can't talk for long, but I'll be home in a couple of days."

She screamed—like a shout for joy. Then she said, "Alex, I can't believe it's you. Oh my God, oh my God, oh my God." She was crying on the other end of the phone. They were happy tears, but it sounded like they were coming out in buckets. She kept saying, "I can't believe it's you."

I said, "I'm coming home, baby. Tell my mother, okay?"

She said, "Thank God, you're okay. Thank God, it's you. Thank God."

I said, "I love you, baby. I'm so, so happy to hear your voice, but I have to go. I'll call when I can."

I ended the call before I was ready, before Alexis was ready. I could have talked to her for hours. But like I said, I didn't want to use up this guy's credits. I didn't think there was any way for him to purchase more out here in the desert, so I tried to do the right thing. But by this time Moustapha had seen me talking and he'd wandered over to ask in on the same deal, and this volunteer worker was too nice to decline. So we used up some more of this poor guy's credits, but he didn't seem to mind.

—⚉—

An hour passed. Then two. Then three. It was now late in the afternoon, and all I'd seen were people coming in to this giant holding area. I hadn't seen anyone leave other than the Egyptian nationals, who were sent directly to the buses outside the compound. As I waited, I struck up a conversation with another Nigerian man. (I could tell he was Nigerian by the color of his passport.) He was traveling with his son and daughter. I said, "My friend, when is our consulate coming?"

He said, "They are not coming." His tone was pleasant, matter-of-fact, resigned.

I said, "What do you mean? They told me it would only be a few hours."

He said, "My friend, I've been here almost ten days. Every day they tell us it will be just a few hours, but no one is coming."

I could not understand this. I could not imagine the load of bureaucratic crap that would keep us waiting in this one room for days and days, but my Nigerian friend explained that this was the situation all along the border. People were risking everything just to get here, seeing themselves through all kinds of danger, just to be warehoused like cattle and fed a bunch of lies and soda and crackers. The United Nations officials, the American embassy, the Nigerian consulate—everybody in charge seemed to want to keep us corralled in these holding cells until the revolution died down, until it was considered safe for us to move about the country.

I just snapped. I'd been wired so tight over the past couple of weeks, completely stressed and horrified and convinced I'd never make it home, that this one piece of frustrating news made me a little crazy. My reaction was totally out of proportion, but I couldn't hold it back, didn't even think to try. This was bullshit, I thought. This was unacceptable. So I marched back out to the last row of booths, towards the guy who'd just stamped my passport and told me someone from the consulate would be by soon, and walked right up to his window. I can't be sure, but I think there was another refugee already standing there, but I didn't care. I probably didn't even notice. I just barged up to the window like a lunatic and started yelling at this dude through the opening in the glass.

I said, "This is bullshit, man. When's the consulate coming? You said it would just be a couple of hours, and now I'm hearing ten days. This is just bullshit."

The guy spoke excellent English, and he didn't exactly appreciate being called out in front of such a big group of weary, worried travelers.

He said, "Sit down, sir. Someone from the consulate will be here shortly."

I was pissed—like over-the-top pissed, and I'm not ashamed to admit it. I said, "Stop with the bullshit, man. We just want to go home. Tell me when the consulate will be here so we can go home."

Once again, the guy asked me to take a seat, but I refused, so he pressed a little button behind his desk, and the next thing I knew, I was surrounded by a half-dozen policemen and soldiers. They took hold of me—one on each arm, another at my waist, another with a tight grip on my neck from behind. Together they pushed me back to the booth, so the guy behind the glass could bark out another batch of orders.

He said, "Passport."

I reached for my Nigerian passport and held it out to him and he grabbed it—just yanked it right out of my hand.

He said, "You'll get this back when the consulate comes."

Then he waved his hand like he was dismissing me, and the soldiers gripping my arms led me downstairs to a small cell behind a heavy steel door that reminded me of the door to my Benghazi apartment. Then they tossed me in and closed the door behind me. It was pitch-black and cold and depressing as hell. They just dumped me there without any explanation—no clue as to how long I'd be held down there, no mention of what I'd done wrong, other than vent a little bit. It's like I was in contempt of court, only instead of being tossed into some holding cell, I was placed in solitary confinement.

This place was eerie, man. Creepy. Like I said, pitch-black. There was no place to sit but the floor. Nothing to do but vent and fume. After a while, I calmed down little by little, and I started to think, *What the hell has happened to me? How did my life get to this point? To be caught in a civil war I can't possibly understand? And now to be imprisoned in a dark, cold cell on the Egyptian border for reasons I can't possibly understand?* I wondered what I'd done, what sequence of events I'd set in motion that had taken me to this time and place, and next thing I knew, I was talking to all these younger versions of myself, like I'd done to pass the time in my Benghazi apartment.

There was no mirror this time. Even if there had been a mirror, I wouldn't have been able to see it. But there was three-year-old Alex, sitting right next to me. There was eight-year-old Alex, all toughened up from playing on our dirt court with my brothers. There was twelve-year-old Alex, finding my way in the States, finding my game. I'd have these full-on conversations, thinking back on things I hadn't thought about in years and years, the whole time saying, "How did we get here, man?" Out loud. Saying, "Where'd we go wrong?" "How can I get back to you guys?"

At one point—I swear it!—I could hear twelve-year-old Alex answer. I could hear him say, "Go back to what you know." As clear as if he'd been right there in that cell with me, which I guess he was.

Go back to what you know.

I talked to myself in this way for a long time. I can't know for sure how long, exactly, but we covered a lot of ground, a lot of deeply weird ground. It's like I'd snapped in some familiar way in that clearinghouse area upstairs, in front of that official in the booth, and now that I was sitting alone in a dark, cold cell, I snapped in a whole other way. I was thinking clearly, though—

clearly enough that I thought maybe I was going crazy—but also clearly enough to know I still had some noise to make if I hoped to get out of there. So what did I do? I made some more noise, man. Big noise. I stood and fumbled for the door and started banging on it, hard. Started yelling, "Get me out of here! Get me the fuck out of here!"

I banged on that door so long, so hard, the heels of my palms turned black-and-blue. After a while, I lost a little steam and sat back down to talk to my younger selves, but then I got fired up all over again and went back to banging and screaming. Back and forth, up and down—this went on for a few hours, I think. Again, it was tough to mark the time, but it felt to me like I was down in that cell for about three or four hours.

Finally, a couple of guards came down, opened the door, and dragged me upstairs. They sat me down in the dirt outside the main building. Apparently, the camp had been slowly and steadily filling up with all these desperate people trying to get into the country, just in the short time Moustapha and I had been there. Folks who'd been there a while had to be pushed outside to make room for the new people coming in. The place was bulging at the seams.

I hooked back up with Moustapha at this point. He'd been worried about me, of course. He was all tense and nervous to begin with, and then to see me hauled away like that . . . all he could think was that I was in some bad, bad shit. So he was pretty happy to see me, and I was pretty happy to see him, and we put our heads together and compared notes. There wasn't much to talk about, really. Our situation hadn't changed all that much, except that we'd been moved outside. Also, we hadn't had anything to eat since the soda and crackers, and we were feeling it. Trouble was, there was no food. A lot of folks had brought their own, had packed a bunch of stuff for their trip to the border, but nobody was willing to share. I actually walked around to all these clusters of people, asking, begging for a bite of food, but people kept shaking their heads, telling me to move on. Telling me, "My brother, I'm sorry, but we only have a small amount. It is just for my family."

I understood that. I did. I was hungry, but I understood that these people had to take care of their kids, so I starting skulking around these big old trash cans that were set up around the grounds. From time to time, people would finish with their food and leave a little bit of meat on the bones of their chicken. There'd be a bite or two of a sandwich or some crumbs bunched up in some wax paper. I was stalking people as they ate, hanging back to see if they'd leave behind any scraps, and then I'd pick through the garbage to see if there was anything I could salvage. That's how hungry I was. That's how desperate.

I didn't want Moustapha to see me like this, so I moved to the other side of the compound to do my begging and foraging. I didn't want *anyone* to see me like this, but of course people noticed. There was this one girl—she must have been about thirteen or fourteen—I caught her staring at me as I shook and flicked a bunch of flies off a mostly eaten chicken leg I'd fished out of the garbage. I must have looked so, so strange to her. On the one hand I was wearing a pair of blue-and-white Kobe Bryant sneakers, a black Nike sweat suit. I wasn't dressed like the kind of person who'd be rooting around in the garbage, but that's just what I was doing. This girl flashed me this look that said, *What's up with that guy?* And for a moment I hated the way I appeared to this girl. But it was survival, man. Survival of the fittest. And this was me, doing what I had to do to make it through.

—〰—

We were stuck in that refugee camp for three days—mostly outside. The whole time, all I had to eat were scraps. The whole time, I didn't sleep. I'd sit up at night and hug my knees and rock back and forth to keep warm. Jesus, it was cold. There were hundreds of people scattered in the dirt surrounding the main processing building, and most of them had blankets, heavy jackets—but they weren't sharing any of this stuff, either. They weren't about to let a six-five black man crawl under their blanket and cuddle up with their family.

Plus, there was a lot of looting going on, a lot of jostling for position and authority. It was haywire. You throw a group of desperate, hungry, tired people together like that and there are bound to be some tensions, some flare-ups, and this was bad upon bad upon bad. People were being robbed. People were being assaulted, attacked for no clear reasons. People were fighting for territory, for little pieces of power, to feel like they were in some kind of control of their fate. It was like being in a prison yard with no guards to watch your back, so Moustapha and I were always careful to keep tabs on each other, on all our stuff, on the other refugees.

We'd pass the night sitting next to each other, keeping close to stay warm. Moustapha managed to sleep in fits and starts, but mostly I sat and hugged my knees and checked out the scene. On the first night, I noticed that one of the gates on the Egyptian side of the compound was unmanned from about three or four in the morning until about six. No guards, no soldiers—nothing. It was the same thing the next night, so I got with Moustapha and told him what I'd seen. Told him how I thought we should make a run for it on the third night, try to jump that gate, maybe see what we could see on the other side. He was reluctant to go against the system—he remembered how I'd been tossed into that cell just for asking a few too many questions a little too loudly—but at the same time, he'd reached a kind of boiling point of his own. He'd had enough.

He was itching to get out of there, same as me.

That whole next day I was wired, felt like I was being watched. And the place was starting to get to me. It takes a lot out of you, trying to remain in a hypervigilant state all the time. Not knowing if the guy next to you is about to jump you. Not knowing when or where you'll find something to eat. Not knowing anything. All of a sudden, everything about this thrown-together camp had me on edge. Even the way we had to go out into a field across from the main area to take a dump struck me as depressing, dehumanizing, dispiriting. There'd be dozens of people out there, right out in the open, men and women and children, just doing their business in this primitive way. It was disgusting, demeaning.

But we had no choice. We were like animals.

That night it started to rain. It came down pretty hard at times. And there wasn't any cover for those of us corralled outside the main building. It just poured and poured right on top of us, soaking through all of our stuff. It had been cold all along, but now it was wet and cold and almost unbearable.

Just before three o'clock that morning, just before the guards were about to abandon their posts according to the schedule I'd mapped out in my head over the past couple of nights, I needed to go to the bathroom. It came on me double-quick, which was weird because I hadn't been eating—but when you've got to go, you've got to go. I told Moustapha I would just run to the field across the way and do my thing and be right back. He said, "You sure you want to go by yourself?"

At night, we thought it was a good idea to move about together, but I figured I could handle a quick trip on my own. The place seemed quiet, dead. No one was moving around in that hard rain. Just to be on the safe side, though, I grabbed one of my knives and slid it into the pocket of my sweats. I also grabbed my travel bag, which I'd taken to carrying at all times, with all my essentials. I'd already been separated from my Nigerian passport, and I didn't want to be without my American passport, my other identification, my wallet, my phone. At all. Ever.

I said, "I'm good, man. I'll just be a minute."

As soon as I got about fifty yards from where we'd been sitting, there was a mess of trees, and I found a bush that would maybe give me a small piece of privacy. It was dark, and there was no one else around, and our dignity had been pretty much stripped away by this point, but I guess old habits are hard to shake. I probably wanted to fool myself into thinking I was civilized or remind myself that I had been, once.

I found a good spot and began to squat to take a dump, but

before I could even get my pants past my waist, I got slammed to the ground—like, ridiculously hard. I didn't know what the hell had hit me at first, but it's like the wind was yanked right out of me. I don't think I blacked out, but I could have. Anyway, I was knocked silly. In all my years playing football, I don't think I'd ever been hit that hard, that unexpectedly, and as I scrambled to catch my bearings and get back on my feet, I saw these two guys in the faint moonlight, coming at me again. It was tough to catch their features, but I could make out their forms. They were big and strong, and it was clear that they meant to do me some serious harm. They came at me again, knocked me back down, and as I wrestled with them in the mud behind this one bush, my eyes began adjusting to the light, and I could see that they were Arab. One of them tried to grab my travel bag, which I held to my chest. The other was trying to get me in a kind of choke hold.

They overpowered me, threw me to the ground, facedown. One of them kicked me in the neck, and as I turned over to try to protect myself, to fight back, the other one landed on top of me and started pummeling me with his fists.

Right away, I thought of the knife in my pocket. Whatever was left of my survival instinct kicked all the way in, and I thought how it would be nothing for me to reach for that knife and stick this guy in the ribs. To cut him into a bloody, hulking pulp. And I could have done it, too. Absolutely, I could have done it. In retrospect, I probably should have. But I didn't. Something held me back, but at the same time another something set me off, and I unleashed this mad fury on the asshole on top of me. I just went completely and totally crazy on him, mostly with my fists. It's like I was lit from within, like I flipped a switch and started screaming, kicking, flailing, punching. I didn't recognize myself, the way I went after this guy. I was like a warrior on tilt. It was almost primal. I scared the crap out of myself, I have to admit—but also, I must have scared the crap out of this guy's partner, because the second guy just took off. He heard his buddy screaming, he heard me screaming, and soon enough he was screaming too, taking off like a chickenshit through another mess of trees.

I'd always been able to protect myself, always been good with my hands, but I was like a madman. I'd been beaten down and weak, but I was filled suddenly with this superhuman strength and fighting spirit, and I just went off. All this rage and fury came tumbling out of me.

Somehow I flipped this guy onto his back and started beating the crap out of him, the whole time thinking about the knife in my pocket. Again, it would have been nothing to dig it out and cut this guy up and finish him off, but instead I finished him off with my fists. It was like I didn't trust myself with the knife, so I put my hands to work instead. Oh, man, I just pounded on this guy. And there was no stopping me. At some point the guy stopped fighting back. He just went limp, but I kept beating on him, pounding on him. There was blood everywhere—all over the ground, all over this guy's face, all down the front of my black Nike warm-up jacket.

I could have killed this guy, the way I went off on him. I could have rained down blow after blow on his head until there was nothing left, but I caught a picture of myself as I was beating on him. It scared me, this roiling rage I'd somehow tapped into—it terrified me, really. In my head, I had this flash of a ten- or twelve-year-old Alex, peering out from behind the bush, looking back at me, seeing what I'd become . . . what *we'd* become. And I didn't like it. It made me sick to my stomach, actually.

How can I get back to you guys?

I stood up and started walking quickly back to camp. The rain was coming down in buckets now, and I was soaked through. The front of my jacket was heavy and thick with this guy's blood. I backpedaled at first, just to keep an eye on my attacker, making sure he didn't get up and follow me, making sure his chickenshit partner didn't emerge from behind some tree and put it all back on me. But this asshole wasn't moving. That other asshole was gone. So I turned and headed back to Moustapha. I stopped by a giant puddle of muddy water and stooped to wash off my face, to splash some water against my clothes, to shake myself back into a feeling somewhat resembling normalcy. And while I was stooping, I thought again of the knife in my pocket, about how I no longer trusted myself to carry a weapon like that, not with the way I'd just gone off on this guy behind the bush.

This wasn't me, I thought. Anyway, this wasn't the me I wanted to be.

I took the knife from my pocket and thrust it into the wet dirt by the puddle and left it there. Then I walked back to Moustapha and sat myself back down next to him. He looked at me funny, like he could maybe tell something had just gone down. He said, "You okay, Alex?"

I said, "I'm okay."

But I wasn't. Of course I wasn't.

I said, "We've got to get out of here."

He said, "Now?"

I said, "Now."

The guards had abandoned their posts, so we grabbed the gear we still had in our possession—in my case, just that small duffel and my backpack-type travel bag with my paperwork, computer, and phone—and made for the gate. We jumped the fence—well, at least we tried to jump the fence. Moustapha cleared it no problem, but I slammed my right thumb on the landing, felt like I might have dislocated it. It hurt like a bitch, but we had no time for me to be hurting like a bitch, so we kept moving, straight to the buses that were lined up on the other side. From where we'd been sitting the past couple of days, we could watch the Egyptian nationals being sent through the gate to board these waiting buses, so we tried to move like we belonged. Like we were going where we had been told.

We walked straight to the first bus and banged on the door, not knowing what we'd find on the other side.

—〰—

The bus driver had been sleeping, we could tell. He rubbed his face, pinched at his eyes. He spoke a little English, enough to know we didn't belong on his bus. Just to confirm what he could tell by looking at us, he stuck out his hand and said, "Passport."

He looked at Moustapha's Senegalese passport, shook his head, handed it back.

He looked at my American passport, shook his head, handed it back.

He said, "I am sorry. Egyptian. Only Egyptian."

Moustapha didn't speak any Arabic, but he was Muslim and thought maybe he could appeal to this guy on some kind of common ground, so he said a few words to the driver in a language I didn't understand.

When Moustapha was finished, the bus driver didn't say anything in response. He just held out his hands, palms up, as if to say, "What can I do?"

I gave it a try, too. I said, "Please, I have to get back to America. We have been through a lot. We only want to get home. Please."

Again, the bus driver didn't say anything, but I could see that he was thinking. I could see that he wasn't holding out his hands—that instead he was weighing a difficult decision. He knew that if he let us on his bus, if he was found out, he could go to prison—or worse. He could jeopardize his whole family. But he also seemed to know that we were desperate, helpless.

Well, God bless this bus driver, because after a long few moments, he waved us toward the back of the bus. He told us to fit ourselves on the floor, wedged between the seats. Then he followed us to the back and reached for a blanket, with which he meant to cover us, only before he shook out the blanket and draped it over us, he held a finger to his lips, like he was reminding us to keep quiet. He said, "Three hours. The bus for Cairo leaves in three hours."

Then he threw the blanket over us and left—probably back to his seat, where he could continue his nap.

Moustapha and I stayed scrunched up like this for a long while beneath the heavy, musty blanket. We spoke quietly to each other for a few moments, talked excitedly about what it might mean to finally make it to Cairo after everything we'd been through, and then I believe we, too, drifted off to sleep. Moustapha, certainly. I could hear his breathing become heavy and steady. I tried to relax, to take my mind away from the bottled-up violence I'd let loose on my attacker in the bushes. I tried to empty my mind, but I don't know if I succeeded. I only know that I was startled from this effort by the sudden ringing of my cell phone from the inside of my travel bag.

Another miracle!

Once again, I'd been checking and checking all along for service. I'd even taken the time to recharge the phone at the desk of the kind young clerk who'd allowed me to borrow his own cell phone to call Alexis in Atlanta. At the time, the clerk thought it strange that I wanted to charge my battery. He said, "Who will you call? You have no credits."

I said, "It is just to be prepared. It is just to keep a full battery."

Apparently, I'd flipped the phone shut the last time I tried to make a call and forgotten to power it down, because here it was, ringing. It took me a long moment to find the phone, but I dug it out soon enough and answered it. It was Coach Sherif, calling from Alexandria. He'd been calling and calling for days and days. He was excited to hear my voice.

He said, "Hey, my boy. How are you doing?"

I said, "Coach Sherif, we are not doing so well. I am with Moustapha. We are under a blanket on the floor of a bus. The driver has agreed to take us to Cairo, but we must be quiet. I cannot really talk. I don't wish to give this man any more trouble than he has already taken on."

He said, "Well, then you must not talk. You must only listen."

Coach Sherif went on to tell me that he and his wife had been praying for us every day since leaving Libya. He apologized for escaping the country ahead of us, explained that it could not be helped. There was a way out, so he took it for the sake of his family. I could understand that, I said. But then Coach Sherif surprised the crap out of me.

He said, "Do you feel like playing a little basketball?"

I wasn't sure I'd heard him correctly. Basketball was about the furthest thing from my mind just then. I hadn't slept in days. I hadn't eaten. Before that, I'd suffered through almost two weeks of absolute hell. I was in no shape to play basketball—to even think about playing basketball. It was so absurd, it hardly rated a response, but I said, "What?"

Coach Sherif explained that a former player of his was now coaching a team in Alexandria—El-Olympi, in the Egyptian League. He said the team was fighting for a playoff spot and could use my help. He said, "It would be good for you, Alex. It would take your mind off of everything that's happened."

I thought, *You have no idea what's happened to me.* I thought, *This is the craziest thing I've ever heard.* But what I said was "Seriously?"

He said, "Yes, seriously. You should not go home just yet. Even if you do not wish to play, you should come to my house in Alexandria. Me and my wife, we will take care of you. You can rest up, gather your strength before you go back to America. You can stay as long as you like."

Before I could answer, he asked if he could speak with Moustapha.

I said, "He is with me right now. He is under the same blanket."

The two of them talked for a while. Coach Sherif told him the same thing and gave the same apology, only to Moustapha, he offered a spot on a team in Cairo.

Like me, Moustapha couldn't believe it. He couldn't even think about playing basketball, and after a few moments, he gave the phone back to me.

Coach Sherif said, "Tell me you will think about it, Alex."

I said, "I will think about it."

He said, "Good."

I said, "Good."

And I was true to my word. I did think about it. Soon it became all I could think about—not basketball so much, but Alexandria. What Coach had said about stopping there to chill for a few days, getting my head back together before going home, seemed to make a whole lot of sense.

Moustapha and I whispered about it underneath the blanket. He was not feeling it the same way I was feeling it. He only wanted to get home. But more and more, I wanted to find a way to get back to how things had been before everything turned to shit. I wanted to lose the image I had of myself, beating my attacker into the ground with my fists. I wanted to shake those thoughts of how easy it would have been to take out my knife and stab that asshole in the chest, over and over. I didn't want to carry any of that home with me. I wanted to return to civilization a civilized man. I'd seen myself as a monster, an animal. I didn't like how I looked, and I thought maybe it would help if I started seeing myself as a basketball player again.

How do I get back to you guys?

We lay there quietly for another hour or so, until I slipped from beneath the blanket to walk to the front of the bus. As I set the blanket back in place, I leaned down to Moustapha and said, "I think I've got to do this, man. I'm sorry."

I thought back to the promise we made to each other in Mr. Ahmed's office, the day we escaped from Benghazi. Where I would go, Moustapha would go; where Moustapha would go, I would go. But we had gotten where we were going, and from here we would go the rest of the way on our own.

We clasped each other by the forearm, a cross between a hug and a handshake. I could not bear the thought of moving on without my good friend, but at the same time, I could not bear the thought of staying on this bus to Cairo. For whatever reason, I'd gotten it into my head that I was meant to go to Alexandria, and once the idea took shape, there was no shaking it. I would see Moustapha again, I felt sure. We would take care of each other in spirit. We would not say good-bye—only "good luck."

The driver had fallen back asleep, so I shook him awake. I said, "Alexandria."

He said, "No, Cairo."

I said, "No, Alexandria." I pointed to myself, and made a *going* motion with my hands. I said, "Me, Alexandria."

He flashed me a look that said, "Man, you're really trying to get me arrested here." Then he threw up his hands, in the style of the region, to show that he was exasperated, but he didn't seem too put out by my request. Only a little bit annoyed. Finally, he stood and opened the door of the bus and began to walk down the steps, motioning for me to follow. He said, "Come."

He ran me across the dirt parking lot to another bus, and he banged on the door for the driver to let us in. From the way the two men spoke, I guessed they were friends. They spoke Arabic—or at least I assumed it was Arabic. As he spoke, the driver pointed to me a couple of times to illustrate whatever point he was trying to make, but as soon as this second driver figured out what his friend was asking, he didn't want me on his bus. He didn't want any trouble.

I reached into my pocket for the rest of my money. I had about $300 left, and I offered it to the driver, but he didn't want to take it. At last he spoke to me in English. He said, "I don't want your money."

And then he waved me towards the back of the bus, but before I walked down the aisle, I took the man's hand, closed it around the wad of bills, and forced him to take it.

At this point, I looked up and saw there'd been fifty sets of eyes on us this whole time. Unlike the bus to Cairo, the bus to Alexandria was full—and it was due to leave in just a few minutes. Moustapha was still sitting by himself, scrunched between the seats at the back of the other bus, covered by a blanket—he wouldn't leave for Cairo for another few hours. But we were about to roll, so I walked down the aisle and tried not to think of all these people looking at me.

I looked like hell. I was soaking wet, muddy, dirty. I wondered if any of these people had seen me coming out of that field just a short time ago with blood on my hands, on my clothes.

There were no empty seats, so I sat down on the floor at the back of the bus, and as we rolled away from the dirt parking area, my heart did a little leap. It felt to me like the worst was past—only it wasn't, not just yet. We came to a stop after just a couple hundred yards.

Another checkpoint.

I tapped the shoulder of one of the passengers in front of me to get his attention. I said, "What is this? Do you know?"

He spoke English, it turned out. He said, "Military."

I sighed—at least I think I sighed, although I cannot be sure if it came across as a sigh of relief or a sigh of worry.

The passenger looked at me and said, "You are from Egypt?"

I said, "No, America."

Quickly, he reached back, put his hand on my head and not-so-gently shoved me beneath his seat. While he was doing this, the bus driver started yelling to the passengers in the back rows. I could not make out what he was saying but imagined he was telling them to find a way to hide me.

Someone produced a blanket and threw it over me, and then someone else draped some carry-on items over the blanket. I was scrunched in a tight ball, positioned in such a way that you could not see my feet from the aisle, and yet I was able to see the feet of the other passengers spilling into the aisle, all the way to the front of the bus. I could see the boots of the guard as he boarded the bus and spoke to the driver. I imagined that he could ask to see everyone's passport or that he could take the driver's word that everyone on board was Egyptian. What I hadn't counted on was something in between: the guard walking down the aisle to the back of the bus, eyeballing the passengers and looking for any suspicious or uncertain behavior.

But that's just what happened, and it was the strangest thing, the way I could follow this man's boots as he did his inspection. I was sweating like a pig under that blanket. The closer he got, the more certain I was that he would stop and pull off the bags and the blanket and haul my ass to jail. Finally, he reached the back of the bus, just across from where I was hiding. I could see him pause for a long beat, and then his boots did a little quarter turn, and then another quarter turn, and he headed back up the aisle, the way he'd come in.

The passengers were dead silent as the guard stepped off the bus, and they remained silent as the driver closed the door and continued on his way, but soon there was a murmuring that seemed to flow from the front of the bus to the back. It reached me like a wave—a wave of good feeling.

The Egyptian man who'd taken the lead in helping me to hide reached back and tapped me on the shoulder.

"America," he said. "Come out."

NINE | ALEXANDRIA

I WAS BURSTING WITH MY STORY, and on the seven-hour drive to Alexandria, it came pouring out. All of a sudden, I had a busload of new Egyptian friends—almost all of them men—and they wanted to hear what I'd been through. A great many spoke English, and the ones who didn't got the translated version from the folks sitting next to them.

As soon as I told my new friends I'd played basketball for Al-Nasr, they wanted to know what I'd been doing since the revolution. They were basketball fans, a lot of them. They wanted to know about this or that player, this or that game. Plus, they wanted to know how things were in Benghazi. They wanted to know if I was coming to play basketball in Egypt.

I said, "There is no more basketball for me right now. I am going home."

One of them said, "Home to America? Then you should be going to Cairo. You do not go to Alexandria if you are going home to America. You are on the wrong bus."

I said, "No, I am going to visit my coach. He will take care of me for a few days."

There was a lot of talking, a lot of celebrating. It wasn't just me who was going home, it was everyone. Each person on that bus had a story. Each person was escaping from some terrible ordeal, anxious to reunite with friends and family, with the people they loved.

After about two hours, the bus pulled over so that the men could pray and get something to eat. We did this a few times. At each rest stop, there was a prayer room and a modest takeout-style restaurant, only I had no money to buy any food. I had a credit card, but there was no ATM, no way to pay electronically. I'd given all my money to the driver from Benghazi, to this bus driver from Sallum. The first time we stopped, I sat off to the side by myself. I did not want to disturb the prayers, and I did not want to sit too close to all of that food since I was so hungry, but one guy all but picked me up off the floor and brought me to where he was sitting. He said, "Come. Eat."

He offered me some chicken, some rice, some bread. And it was amazing—like, the most amazing food I'd ever tasted. And there was a ton of it. The food just kept coming and coming.

The second time we stopped, I did the same thing. I did not want to take this kindness for granted or seem like I expected it, so I stayed to the side. While the other men prayed, I dropped to my knees in the dirt and prayed as well. My eyes were closed when one of the men came to collect me and asked me to join him and his friends.

I said, "No, that's okay. I'm praying."

He said, "Come. You pray with us."

I said, "I am Christian. I do not pray the same way."

He said, "It is no matter. You still pray with us."

So I did. I said, "Thank you, Lord. Thank you for seeing me safely to this place. Thank you for these men. Thank you."

After we prayed, we ate. This time there was hummus.

I could not believe the warmth and kindness of these good people. It was the most surprising thing, the most wonderful thing, and when we finally got to Alexandria, it was like I was part of a whole new community. I fit myself right in.

I expected Coach Sherif to meet the bus. I'd borrowed a phone from one of my new friends and told Coach I was coming, but I couldn't find him at first, so a few guys offered me a ride. Another few offered to get me a taxi. And another few offered to wait with me, but I kept telling them it was okay, that they had all done enough.

After a while, Coach Sherif pulled up, and the Egyptians descended on his car and gave him their reports. They knew who he was, by reputation. As a coach, Sherif was well known throughout the region—in his home country especially. They spoke to him in Arabic. I had no idea what they were saying, but Coach later told me that they were just telling him that I was okay, that I'd been fed, that they'd looked after me.

In Egypt, they do this thing where you kiss each other on the cheek, twice. So I kissed everyone on the cheek, twice. Thirty men, sixty kisses. Each time, they offered me a prayer in parting. They said things like, "May Allah bless you." They said, "*Hamdullah.*"

They were such good dudes, man—thirty angels sent to guide

me, protect me, feed me. It was ridiculous—like a story out of the Bible.

Coach Sherif and his wife were heaven-sent, too, the way they took me in, cooked for me, made sure I was comfortable. I took a shower, changed my clothes. I had a clean pair of jeans and a couple of clean T-shirts in my duffel. Coach's wife cooked up an incredible feast, and I thought I'd never stop eating. She even took a look at my busted-up thumb, which I'd hurt hopping that fence at the refugee camp, and taped it up like a team trainer.

As soon as I could, I set up my laptop and talked to my girl on Skype. I didn't want to be rude and disappear on my hosts as soon as I walked in the door, but I was itching to talk to Alexis. It was getting late in Alexandria, probably after midnight, but it was a good time to call the States. I knew it'd probably been tough on Alexis, not knowing what was going on with me, if I was dead or alive, so I wanted to make sure we had a good chunk of time to talk. We had a lot of ground to cover. We hadn't gotten too far on that first call back at the refugee camp, because we were both crying so much. I don't even remember much of what we said. Now that we were on Skype, Alexis started checking me out, started telling me I wasn't looking so hot. She said, "You've lost a lot of weight, Alex. I'm worried about you."

She was right to worry. I'd lost about twenty pounds, but I told her I was okay. And I was.

She said, "You don't look like yourself."

Again, she was right. I didn't. My hair was wild. My beard was sprouting up all over the place. I was a mess. But I said, "It's me under all this hair. Don't worry."

We probably talked for about twenty minutes that night—and

then, as soon as we signed off, I called my mother. Alexis had been in touch with her right after that call I'd made a couple of days earlier, so she knew I was okay; she knew I was headed home. Still, she was overjoyed to hear from me, almost like she couldn't believe it until she heard from me directly.

I knew from Alexis that my mother had gone ballistic on the State Department, trying to track me down. I knew she went off on a whole bunch of people—but hey, that's just my mother, looking out for me. I started off by teasing her a little about that, telling her I'd heard she made all kinds of trouble for me. But then she slammed me with some news about my father, told me he wasn't doing so hot. This hit me by surprise. Alexis hadn't really said anything—we were so busy crying and reconnecting and talking about my dramatic weight loss—but my mother gave it to me straight, said my father wasn't reacting all that well to his latest round of chemo. She said his blood sugar was up, that he was struggling.

She said, "The doctor just told him to lay off the chemo for two weeks, to give his body a chance to get right."

That pissed me off, to be completely honest. That was my first thought—not the healthiest reaction, I confess, but I want to tell it straight. I mean, after slogging through all the shit I'd had to slog through those past couple of weeks: Being held at gunpoint. Nearly starving to death. Having to deal with all that bloodshed and brutality happening right in front of me. Not knowing if I'd make it out of Benghazi alive. To go through all of that only to hear that my dad's diabetes had taken a turn for the worse, that he wasn't responding to his chemo . . . well, it set me off. I couldn't take it, and I think some of that anger spilled out into this one Skype call with my mother. As soon as it did, I instantly regretted that I'd let her see me so upset. I needed to be strong for her, to help her through what she had to do for my dad, but I was weak, vulnerable. That's why I was so pissed, I think— because I was so weak, so beaten down by the horrors of the past couple of weeks. I just couldn't deal.

After a while, I told my mom I had to sign off. Told her I'd probably sleep for the next fifteen hours. I was beat—and Coach Sherif and his wife had me set up in a sweet, comfortable room with a big old bed and nice, clean sheets. It's like the bed was calling to me from across the room. I'd been up for days and days, didn't think I could keep my eyes open much longer, so I told my mother I loved her and I'd call her the next afternoon.

I hit the pillow and was out cold.

—w—

The next morning, I woke up late—it was probably already afternoon. I couldn't remember the last time I'd had such a good sleep. Coach Sherif was waiting for me when I got up. He couldn't have been nicer, more generous. He kept telling me how awful he'd felt, ducking out of Benghazi that first day. He kept telling me he'd been praying for me—for all his players, but for me and Moustapha most of all. He said, "The Libyans, they would find their way around. But for you, it could not have been easy."

As he spoke, I started thinking of that line I used to hear all the time from Coach West at Alcorn State. *If you put me one hundred miles in the desert, I will come back to you with a bucket of chicken and a milkshake.* For the first time, I thought I understood what he meant. It was a message about faith and loyalty—in this case, about Coach West's faith and loyalty to his players. And here, now, Coach Sherif was telling me how he'd been reaching out to us since the moment he'd had to flee, that he could not rest until Moustapha and I were safe.

Coach Sherif wasn't pressing me to talk, to unload what I'd been going through onto him, but I knew that he was available if that's what I wanted. I understood that he'd been truly conflicted about leaving us behind, and I couldn't hold that against him. We'd always been close, me and Coach Sherif. Almost as soon as I'd gotten to Benghazi, as soon as I'd gotten to know him, the revolution in Egypt had started to take shape, so Coach Sherif was anxious about the situation back home. He was down a lot of the time, especially as the peaceful protests turned violent. His head wasn't always in the game, and Moustapha and I used to sit with him and try to pick him up. We'd tell him, "Everything will be okay." We'd say, "We'll play for your family." As if we had any idea. As if playing for his family made any difference.

Yeah, he'd fled Libya at his first chance, so he couldn't really know how things were for us in the heart of Benghazi, in the heart of the revolution. But I understood that he'd only left to get back to Alexandria, to see his family, his countrymen through their own revolution. As much as anyone else I was likely to meet from here on in, Coach Sherif knew how it was, and we got to talking. That first afternoon, it all came out. We talked and talked. It was March 6—a Sunday—seventeen days after the first blood had been shed in the streets of Benghazi, and I told Coach Sherif everything. I told him about the soldiers

gunning down all those protesters with a rifle mounted on that
SUV. Told him about the little girl dragging her father's body
through the town square, leaving a heartbreaking trail of blood
behind him. Told him about my neighbor, all but beaten to death
in the stairwell outside my apartment while his daughter was
being brutally raped just a few feet away. Told him about the
mini mercenaries who helped get me out of the city, and the rebel
guards who'd come *this close* to killing Moustapha at that first
checkpoint on our way out of town.

I stopped short of telling him how I went off on my attacker
in the bushes at the refugee camp in Sallum, because I didn't like
how that story made me look. I didn't understand it, didn't think
I ever would, and wanted more than anything to wish it away.
Mostly, I couldn't recognize the cold-blooded, half-crazed, hard-
hearted animal I'd become in that moment.

So I left all of that out when I talked to Coach Sherif that first
day in Alexandria. Told him everything else, though. Told him
about my father's diabetes, about how the chemo that was supposed to save him might be killing him instead. Told him more,
probably, than he needed to hear. But he hung with me. He didn't
flinch. And when I was finished, he put his arm around me and
said, "You've been through a lot, Alex." That's all—just "You've
been through a lot."

I thought, *Yes. Yes, I have.*

He said, "I want you to play for my friend here in Alexandria."

I said, "Basketball? You want me to play basketball?"

He said, "It will be good for you, I think. You need something to take your mind off what you've been through. You need
a new focus."

I said, "I need to get home. I need to catch a train to Cairo and a flight back to the States."

He was a smart man, Coach Sherif. And a persistent man. He wanted what was best for me, but at the same time he wanted what he wanted, and after a couple of hours, he convinced me that I could not go back to Alexis so soon after the things I'd just seen, the things I'd just experienced. I could not go back to my family. He was afraid I might snap. He said, "Doctors, they call this post-traumatic stress disorder. Perhaps this will happen to you. Perhaps this is what is happening to you already. Perhaps it is best if you give yourself some time before you go home, if you give yourself something to do."

The more I thought about it, the more it made sense. I didn't know how in the world I'd sell it to Alexis or to my parents, but it made sense. Coach Sherif was right: I was too raw, too shaken, too flattened to see any of them just yet. Too far away from the person I'd been—and still too close to the person I'd become. I could have killed a man with my bare hands. This was a huge thing to consider. I'd been talking to myself out loud, in a full-on delusional way. I couldn't carry all that shit home with me, so we talked more and more about basketball.

It was easy, familiar.

El-Olympi was a good team in a competitive twelve-team league. The top six teams made it to the playoffs, and El-Olympi was fighting for the sixth and final spot. There were only ten games left in the season, so it's not like Coach was asking me to sign on for a six-month stint. At most, it would be about six weeks—maybe a little bit longer if the team made a deep playoff run.

The way it works in the Egyptian League is that each team is

allowed to make one international player change during the season. El-Olympi had a foreign player go home during the team's
Christmas break, and the dude never came back. Coach Sherif
said he was homesick. And now here it was a couple of months
later, and the team still hadn't refilled its international player spot.
That's why Coach Sherif thought it might be a good fit for me.
Plus, they needed a guard who could play the point, who could
shoot, defend, distribute—all the things I did in my sleep, when
I was right.

El-Olympi was hanging on, playing competitive ball, so they
had a decent enough team even without this one player, and once
Coach laid it all out for me, it started to get my competitive juices
flowing again. I started to think that I could maybe be a part of
something pretty cool, maybe take my mind off the hell of the past
weeks, get my head in a more positive place before returning home.

That's how I was leaning, anyway, only I told Coach Sherif I'd
have to talk to Alexis before I could commit to playing. I'd have
to talk to my parents, too. Those were tough calls to make. How
do you tell your girlfriend who kind of/sort of thought you were
maybe/possibly dead for a couple of weeks that you won't be coming home for a couple of months more? How do you tell your
father who might be dying that you're choosing to stay half a
world away over coming home to be at his side? Because you want
to stay and play *basketball*? There's no script for that kind of
conversation—and even if there had been a script, no one at home
would have followed it.

Alexis went off on me. She said, "Alex, you must have lost
your damn mind!" She said, "I'm gonna fly over there and whoop
your ass myself!"

It was bad. I think she hung up on me the first time I put it to her.

It didn't go over any better with my mother. She said, "You know what this will do to your father?" She said, "This will kill him."

My brothers, my sisters—they didn't want me to stay, either. They all thought I was nuts. And who knows, maybe I was. The news out of Egypt was no better than the news out of Libya—at least the way it was being reported back home. But here in Alexandria, it did not feel to me like the city was under siege. The protests were mostly nonviolent. The people were going about their daily business, same as before.

It was not like Benghazi.

My mother actually called Coach Sherif herself to get his take. She knew he and I were close. She knew he had my back. She knew me well enough to know I wouldn't make a decision like this recklessly, heartlessly, so she gave me that benefit of the doubt. But at the same time she wanted to hear what Coach had to say.

He said, "Your son, he's not right. The things he's seen, nobody should have to see. The things he's done, nobody should have to do. He needs to be someplace where he can rest and reflect."

She thought this made a certain amount of sense. Not a lot, but some. She said, "He can do those things at home. Why does he need to play basketball?"

Coach Sherif said, "He does not *need* to play basketball, Mrs. Owumi. That's like an extra. I believe it will help him to play. It will help set his mind right. He does not need to play, of course. If he likes, he can just stay with me and rest. But to go home is a mistake, I think."

My mother was not convinced, but she appreciated Coach Sherif's concern.

My father did not offer an opinion. I spoke to him only briefly about the situation, and he could only offer his standard line. He said, "If it's good for you, it's good for me." Same thing he always said about everything—but this time I was starting to think he was right.

—⟋⟍⟍—

Alexis wouldn't come around. Not for a while. She was pissed, wouldn't even talk to me at first, but she had a couple of long talks with my mother, and the two of them must have come to some sort of understanding. It's not like they decided to agree with me on this or even to support my decision, but there was a kind of truce. What's that term they use in international relations? A *détente?* Well, that's where we got to soon enough. We agreed to disagree. My two women, they backed off, almost like they took up my father's position. Almost like they'd just set the whole thing aside.

If it's good for you, it's good for me.

Later that first day, Coach Sherif got through to Moustapha, who'd made it to Cairo and was waiting for a flight back to Senegal. This was welcome news. Ever since Moustapha and I had parted so suddenly on that bus in Sallum, it felt like I was leaving a piece of myself back in the desert. Like there was unfinished business. I could not feel like I had been delivered into a place of safety and certainty without knowing that Moustapha, too, was in a good place, and I was so overwhelmed with feelings of relief and gratitude that my good friend was out of danger that I dropped to my knees and gave thanks.

Also, Coach Sherif asked Tarek Sobhi to come by to meet me. Tarek used to play for Coach Sherif, and now he was carving out his own career as a coach. He struck me right off as a good guy. He understood what I'd been through. He understood that I'd lost a lot of weight, that I'd need to play myself back into shape—all of that. And he understood the game, made me feel like the team really needed me. This last point was key, because Tarek had never seen me play. He was going on Coach Sherif's recommendation—but that was enough, apparently. He offered me a nice deal: $9,500 per month for the balance of the season, including the playoffs, plus another $9,500 bonus if we wound up winning the whole thing, not to mention the game bonuses I could collect along the way, which could run to $300 or $400 per game.

The money had never been a part of my thinking, but once Tarek put it out there, it was too rich to ignore. With success, I stood to make as much as $40,000—big money at that time in my life, that time in my career. And I'd bring it all home with me, too, because the team would put me up in a nice apartment. I'd have to pay for my own food, but groceries were cheap in Alexandria, and there were team meals every here and there, so I wouldn't have to dig too deep into my own pockets.

After this one meeting with Tarek, I agreed to attend a team practice the following afternoon, to see what I could see. I'd lace up and run with the team, but it was understood that it wasn't any kind of audition. I was weak and out of shape and probably rusty as hell, so it was more a chance for me to check out my potential future teammates and the El-Olympi operation than it was a chance for them to see what I could do.

Alexis still wasn't all the way on board with the way I was leaning on this, but at least she'd stopped telling me I was fucking crazy.

I'd been eating like a linebacker since arriving in Alexandria. I was determined to gain back the weight I'd lost, and right away. Trouble was, I wasn't always so smart about what I ate or when I ate it. The next day, I hit a McDonald's on the way to my first El-Olympi practice. That's always a fool move, but when you eat as much as I was determined to eat, it's a damn fool move. Here's what I ordered: two Double Quarter Pounders with Cheese, a large fries, two apple pies, and a large chocolate shake. That's a couple of pounds of food right there. An hour later, I was sick as a dog, threw it all up, but I still had to go to this practice. Tarek ran us hard, and I couldn't keep up. I'd thought my busted-up thumb might give me some trouble, but that turned out to be okay—it was the least of my problems. The guys on the team, they'd heard I was a good player, but they couldn't tell it from this first session. They couldn't tell because I could hardly make it up and down the court. I couldn't play a whiff of defense, couldn't beat anyone off the dribble . . . basically, I couldn't do shit. And after an hour or so, these guys were all scratching their heads, wondering what the hell I was doing there.

I can't say I blamed them.

They were good dudes, my prospective teammates. They didn't take advantage of me the way they might have or try to show me up in any way, but at the same time, they didn't get how I could possibly be the guy who would help lift them into the playoffs. As far as they could see, I couldn't even lift my own feet off the floor.

A few of the players on the team spoke English, and one of them came up to me during a break. At first I thought he was just being friendly, just trying to welcome me to the group—and I guess he was, but there was more to it than that. He said, "My friend, I have seen you play on television. What happened?"

Meaning, how did my game go from all the way up there, on television, to all the way down here, where it was right now?

I said, "I've been through something."

That's all I would cop to. I didn't want them to know my story, didn't want to make excuses, so every time it came up, I just said, "I've been through something."

After that first practice, I decided to stay on. I couldn't face going home, not just yet. It felt to me like I still needed to decompress a little after what had gone on in Libya, and competitive basketball was a good distraction.

My first game with El-Olympi was against Tanta, a team near the bottom of the standings, so it was a game we expected to win. It was also a game we needed to win if we wanted to make the playoffs. Essentially, we had to run the table to assure a postseason berth, and this was our first test. The thing is, a lot of the international referees don't like it when the game is a blowout, and it was looking like this was very much the case here in Egypt. We jumped out to a big lead, but by the start of the second half, there were so many questionable calls against us that Tanta was able to close the gap.

I played okay. I'd had only three or four practices by this point, so I was nowhere near full strength, and I still hadn't learned my teammates and their tendencies, which has always been a big part of my game. Tarek left me in the whole way, which he didn't have to do, but which I certainly appreciated. I needed to get those minutes in my legs, to get my wind back.

It was a home game for us—only we didn't exactly have a home court. We played at Alexandria Stadium, which holds about ten thousand, but the games don't really sell out until the playoffs—and the fans who do show up aren't always pulling for El-Olympi. For a regular-season game like this one, the place was maybe half full, so it wasn't a pumped-up environment, but I was cool with that for the time being. I thought it made sense to work the kinks out, to get back in shape, before playing in front of a big, big crowd.

We won that first game, and the game after that, and the game after that. Each time out, I played a little better, felt a little stronger. Each time out, my teammates found something new to like in my game, a few more reasons to believe in me and what I could do—and in turn, I saw things in their games to admire. My shots started to fall. My passes found their marks. Even the fans in Alexandria were starting to lean our way. Best of all, my postgame Skype sessions with Alexis were getting a little better, a little warmer. She was beginning to understand why I'd needed to stay on in Alexandria for a bit, to get my head straight. Also, the more we talked, the more she let on one of the main reasons she was so upset with me when I first floated the idea. After what she and her family had been through with Hurricane Katrina, she realized how short life can be. In her eyes, faith and family are all you've got, and here it felt to her like I was putting my career in front of all my loved ones. She thought I was making a selfish decision, and on top of that, it felt to her like she was losing the most important man in her life all over again. Also, it left her feeling like she wasn't important enough for me to hurry on home to, like things weren't so serious between us. But it wasn't like that at all. It took a while, but soon Alexis was able to see that, and soon after that we were good.

One of the things that dogged me the whole rest of the season was the way my new teammates liked to goof around when they had the lead. They'd showboat or strut, which isn't the smartest approach when you're playing in a league where the refs are out to keep the games close. I'd only been there a short while, but I rode my guys hard about this. Yelled my head off at times, which was probably stupid, because most of my teammates couldn't understand a word I was saying. But my big thing has always been that no lead is safe. Five points, ten points, twenty points—it's never enough. Basketball is a game of runs. It's a game of three-pointers, good possessions. These guys didn't really understand that. We'd go up by ten points, late, and my teammates would get all loose and careless. They'd play like they were already celebrating, but all that had to happen was for the other team to put together two or three strong possessions, follow each one with a stop, and they'd be back in the game.

Either you take the game seriously or you don't.

Our big rival was a team called Etisalat, which was sponsored by the main cell phone company in Egypt. They weren't the best team in the league that year, but they were probably the most successful sporting club in the country. They were like the New York Yankees, like Manchester United. Always, they were the team to beat, and we had a rivalry with them going back years and years. It actually started as a soccer rivalry, and they were generally regarded as the most dominant club in the Egyptian Premier League, but it had now spilled over into basketball.

We went to Cairo to play them on their home court, and the atmosphere was completely different than it was for us in Alexandria Stadium. Really, it was tremendous. The Etisalat fans were over the top. The arena was just nuts, but we took it to them that night. Like all our games down the stretch that year, it was a game we had to win—and at one point, we were up more than twenty points. But then the questionable calls started to go against us, and somehow the refs managed to even things out. It wasn't all on the officiating, the way this one game turned, but it didn't help that every damn whistle went the other way.

Etisalat was led by an American player named Brian Edwards, a six-seven power forward who had played his college ball at Miami of Ohio. He'd been playing in Egypt for a bunch of years, so he knew the league, he knew the players, he knew the refs. I'd just been there a couple of weeks, and even I knew that if the refs were trying to tilt the game back your way, it probably wasn't a good idea to question any one call. The thing to do was just to roll with whatever the refs called and know that you'd have a chance to compete at the end.

That's just how this one game was playing out. We had been up big, but then the refs had helped to whistle Etisalat close to even. With about a minute to go in the game, we were up by a single point. We'd been up by seven moments earlier, but Etisalat hit back-to-back threes to make it close. So on our next possession, I drove the lane and hoped for a foul or an easy basket. I got a little more than that. The ref called a foul on Brian Edwards as

I went up for a layup—although, to tell the truth, the guy never touched me. I missed the layup, but the game turned on this one play because it was Brian Edwards's fifth foul. In Egypt, same as in a lot of international leagues, you only get five personal fouls, so he was out of the game—and as soon as the ref made the call, Brian went ape shit. He charged at the ref and started yelling at him, bumping him, the way you sometimes see a baseball manager go chest to chest with an ump at home plate. Naturally, the ref strung him up with a technical. This set Brian off even more, so he started cursing and throwing things. And when the dust finally cleared, I was sent to the line to shoot *five* free throws—two from the original shooting foul and three technicals.

Five free throws!

Edwards was fuming. He was jumping up and down, saying, "That's bullshit! That's bullshit!"

And it was—complete and total bullshit. I'd missed a gimme layup, that's all. There wasn't any contact. But the ref had the whistle and this was his call.

All I could do was laugh—and as Brian left the court, I walked past him to see if maybe I could calm him down, maybe get him to laugh about it, too. (Yeah, we were opponents, but we were also Americans, so we had to stick together.) I said, "Take it easy, man. No big thing. We get our checks tomorrow either way."

I can't be sure, but I think this set him off even more.

Let me tell you, it was one of the craziest things I'd ever seen on a basketball court.

It would be nice to report that I sank all five shots to put the game away, but that's not exactly how it happened. What happened was I only hit three of the five free throws, which was kind of terrible in terms of shooting percentage, but it gave us enough of a margin that we were able to hold on and win.

Heading into the final game of the season, we'd won nine straight. We'd clinched a fifth-place finish overall, so our last game didn't mean all that much. Tarek took the opportunity to rest his regulars, but we almost won the game anyway—that's how well we were playing down the stretch. It's like we couldn't lose.

The way it works in the Egyptian league is the top two teams draw a bye in the first round of the playoffs, so the third- and sixth-place teams and the fourth- and fifth-place teams play each other in best-of-three series. The games are played in neutral-site arenas, which worked out great for us because we didn't have much of a fan base in Alexandria, so we weren't giving up any kind of home-court advantage.

We had such momentum that we breezed right past our first- and second-round opponents to make it to the finals against Al-Ittihad, a big-budget, big-time team, also from Alexandria. Like El-Olympi, they'd lost their international player during the run of the season—Darren Kelly, a guard from the University of Texas—but they'd never gotten around to filling his spot on the roster. Still, they were pretty damn deep without him. They were led that year by a six-nine national team player named Ismail Ahmed. This guy was unbelievable—probably one of the best players in the Middle East. He had big hands, could shoot the three, was an outstanding ball handler. And he was surrounded by some really, really good players—like, four or five other national team players, so they had a lot of talent.

They were the heavy favorites going into the series, which meant we were the heavy fan favorites. One thing I'd learned about Egyptian sports fans was that they love to root for the underdog. It was almost a national pride thing with them—especially now that the people had banded together to protest the oppressive regime of longtime Egyptian president Hosni Mubarak. There was, like, an us-versus-them, David-versus-Goliath mentality in the streets, and it seemed to fill the arena as well. We were the little guys in this matchup. We were the giant-killers.

Al-Ittihad had a bunch of different ways to beat us, up and down the bench, but we were playing out of our heads. We were on fire. I'd been playing some of the best ball of my career. I didn't really realize it while it was happening, but looking back, I can see it was a great run for me. Coach Sherif had been right to encourage me to finish out the season here. My head was finally in a good place—my body, too. I wasn't back to whole—not by a long stretch—but I was getting back to normal, on the court and off. It had been more than six weeks since Benghazi, and I'd put back all the weight I'd lost, shaken most of the rust from my game. I thought back to that great piece of advice I'd gotten from my coach, Jerry Burns, when I was playing at Monroe Community College, when he'd looked at me in the mirror and said, "You've got to practice harder."

And so I did.

Most important, there were a bunch of guys on our team who really complemented my style of play. Tarek had us running the floor like we'd been playing together a couple of years instead of just a couple of months, so we were all really feeling it, all at the same time. That's how it goes sometimes in the game of basketball. One player gets hot, the rest of the team gets hot right along with him. You're on fire together.

In Game One of the three-game series, we took it to them. I scored twenty-eight points, which was a big number for me—a big number for a forty-minute game—but the bigger deal was the way we were moving the ball as a team. It wasn't any kind of blowout. Al-Ittihad was too good, too deep for that, but we controlled the game the whole way. The outcome was never in doubt, so in that sense it was a dominant performance for us as a team. It sent us looking ahead to the next game with a whole lot of confidence.

Our goal was to win the championship in back-to-back games. We didn't want to let Al-Ittihad back into the series and send it to a deciding game, so we were really up for the next game. All the way up. Our guys were loose, focused, determined—all at once. But then something happened to knock me down from my pregame high. All the way down.

I was in the arena, going through my usual pregame ritual, calling home on Skype to my girlfriend, my parents, whoever I could find online. I called so they could wish me luck, so I could put my mind in a positive place. So there I was, sitting on the floor just outside the locker room, wearing my big old headphones, talking to my mom, and I could hear it in her voice that something wasn't right. I couldn't think what it was, so I just put it to her. I said, "Mom, what's wrong?"

She could never lie to me. She could avoid telling me something, which in her mind was completely different, but she could never flat-out lie to one of her kids, so she came right out with it. She started to cry a little bit, said, "It's your father, Alex. He's in a diabetic coma."

I said, "Holy shit, Mom. Why didn't you tell me? When did this happen?"

She said, "Five days ago."

I couldn't believe it. I said, "Five days ago? And you didn't tell me?"

She said, "I'm sorry, but I didn't want to worry you. All of us, we didn't want to worry you. There's been so much on your plate."

I was devastated, completely floored. My mom talked to me for a bit about what this meant for my dad, about what the doctors were saying, about what we could expect to happen next. But underneath all of that, I was also pretty upset that something like this could be going on all the way back home, and no one in my family had thought to fill me in. I was caught between concern and outrage.

We had a good cry together and propped each other up as best we could, but we ended the call before long. We were both too shaken to keep talking. But before I went back to the locker room to join my teammates, I called my brothers. They told me the same thing, that they didn't want to worry me, that I'd been through enough. Just a whole bunch of bullshit, you know? "All of us, we didn't want to worry you," one of them said. I thought, *What the hell is that?* It felt to me like one giant conspiracy. And they wouldn't even talk to Alexis that whole time—they were all avoiding her calls because they knew she'd be on Skype right away, filling me in.

They couldn't lie to her, and she couldn't lie to me.

It is a devastating thing to hear, that your dad is in a diabetic coma, so when I put away my laptop, my head was all over the place. It was everywhere but on the game we were about to play. I was angry that my family thought they had to tiptoe around me on this. But at the same time, I was also feeling guilty that I'd put off going home to stay on in Egypt for a couple of months—a couple of months I could have spent with my dad. Mostly, I was feeling sad and frustrated and overwhelmed . . . all bundled up together in a tight emotional ball.

As soon as I went back into the locker room, all those emotions came rolling on out of me. I took one look at my teammates, horsing around, getting loose, singing, laughing, dancing, and I went off on them. I just popped. I kicked the door, slammed my hand into one of the lockers, screamed. After that, it's like a slow-rolling wave washed over the locker room, and one by one the guys quieted, started looking at me funny. They'd never seen me like this, had no idea what to make of it—and now that I'd apparently gotten their attention, I had no idea what to tell them, if I should even say anything at all.

Someone turned down the music, so I took the opportunity to grab one of my teammates, Mohamed Adly, who happened to speak very good English. (He also happened to be standing right next to me.) I said, "Mohamed, help me out, man."

He said, "What?"

I said, "Can you translate for me?"

He nodded. And then I just started talking and talking. Told the whole story of my time in Libya, my escape from Benghazi, my struggles in that refugee camp in Sallum . . . everything. It was the flip side of all those times I kept putting people off, pushing them away, saying, "I've been through something." This was what I'd been through. This was what I'd asked Tarek not to share, and it all came tumbling out of me. I didn't tell the whole story, of course. There wasn't really time for that. But I gave them the edited version. I told them why I'd been so gaunt, so frail when I joined the team, why I was always racing to the bathroom to throw up, why I had to keep taking all those parasite pills. I told them everything, up to and including this latest news from home about my father.

Mohamed, he stayed with me. He took what I was saying and put it back out into the room in a way my teammates could understand. By the time I was through, I was crying—and this part didn't have to be translated. The guys could all see how broken up I was. It was all so *right there*, man. And once I'd said what I had to say, I was drained. Spent. You know how you hear people talk about the times they open themselves up and share a great burden and it feels like a great weight has been lifted? Well, this wasn't like that at all. This just felt like I'd now brought this good group of guys into my misery, that's all. I didn't feel any lighter or better or more hopeful. None of that. All I felt was finished, done.

Playing for the championship of the Egyptian League was about the last thing on my mind.

For a few long moments, the locker room was mostly silent. But after a while, a couple of the guys started whispering to each other, murmuring. After another while, their words reached the front of the room, where I'd been standing with Mohamed Adly. I could not think of anything else to say. I did not know what to do next. But Mohamed Adly, he knew. He heard his teammates, and he knew. He turned to me and said,

"Alex, we will play this game for your father. We will win this game for your father."

It was the most remarkable thing. And these guys were true to their pledge. They played like world-beaters, man. I had no energy, could barely focus, but my teammates played their asses off. It was ridiculous. Diving for loose balls. Flying out-of-bounds to keep a ball in play. Slapping each other on the back, saying, "Come on! Come on!" Talking some sick trash to the other team—they were just relentless.

I looked on and thought, *Damn, where have you guys been?*

Even with my teammates playing out of their heads like that, we led by only one point at halftime. They'd played their best and still we were barely ahead, so I knew I'd have to kick a little something into the mix if we expected to keep Al-Ittihad on its heels in the second half. They were too good to keep down for too long. Plus, I figured my guys would be exhausted after the way they'd played their hearts out. I didn't think they'd have much left in the tank, so I dialed in. I set aside my worries about my dad and tried to focus on the game.

Yeah, I know, I should have been focused all along. I was a professional basketball player, right? But it had all been so raw back when we'd started the game. I'd just heard this killer piece of news from home, so it took me a while to get my head around that. It took me a while to get it going—but I had to get it going.

I was here, after all. It was time to get into the game.

Either you take the game seriously or you don't.

The second half was a fight on both sides of the ball. We traded the lead a couple of times. Our guys were a little gassed after that extra effort in the first half, and the Al-Ittihad players were a little amped, knowing their season was on the line. These two truths kind of balanced each other out, and each side was looking for some way to tilt things back in its favor.

We were down four, late, when Coach Tarek had an idea. There was less than a minute to go in the game, so it was a desperation-type move—one I didn't fully agree with at first, but he didn't ask my opinion and I didn't offer it. He called on one of our little guys, Mohamed Ganesh, to come in off the bench. Mohamed Ganesh was five-six, usually played the point when I needed a breather, but here we would both be on the floor at the same time. I couldn't understand Tarek's thinking on this. I thought we needed to get big, not small, but Coach had a different thought. He later told me that he wanted to throw Al-Ittihad a different look, with two point guards, maybe put them on their heels. Mohamed Ganesh was a scrappy player. Athletic, but also crazy. Unpredictable. He had a habit of taking the worst shots at the worst possible times—but he was also like a spark plug. Sometimes those terrible shots would fall, and the entire game would turn. Other times he would find a way to make something happen, and I guess that's what Tarek was hoping for here.

Sure enough, Mohamed made a play as soon as he entered the game. The man he was guarding was dribbling the ball at mid-court, nonchalantly, and Mohamed just kind of leaned in and swiped it from him, then drove the length of the floor for a gimme layup.

Now we were down just two, but there were only ten or twelve seconds left to play. Al-Ittihad inbounded the ball beneath its own basket—a tough assignment in a tight game. In the international game, you can't advance the ball to half-court after a made basket by calling a time-out the way you can in the NBA, so this gave us a bit of an edge. They had the ball, but we had momentum coming off that careless turnover, and now we were piling on the pressure. The ball came in to Al-Ittihad's big man, a seven-footer, and little Mohamed Ganesh was the closest defender. Right away, Coach Tarek started screaming at Mohamed from the bench to give a foul. Realistically, that was our only hope, to send this guy to the line and pray he'd miss at least one shot to give us a chance to tie the game.

Mohamed didn't foul, so Coach yelled at him again, but instead our little guy was just swarming around their big guy— tying him up, playing regular defense. That wasn't what the situation called for, and it had the big guy confused. And then, just when Tarek was about to bust a vein from yelling at Mohamed to give a foul, Mohamed lunged for the ball and stripped it right out of the big man's hands. He was standing directly under our basket, so Mohamed went straight up with it. For a moment it looked like the big man would swat the ball out of the air, but Mohamed slipped into highlight-reel mode. Oh, man, it was something to see. He went up with his right hand, switched to his left, and kind of scooped the ball beneath the outstretched arms of Al-Ittihad's frustrated big man for the prettiest layup I'd ever seen. Plus, Mohamed was fouled on his way down, the big man knocking him to the floor. So now the game was tied and Mohamed, our spark plug, was headed to the line with a chance to put us in the lead with about three seconds left on the clock.

Coach Tarek went off a little bit on our sideline. He was jumping up and down, hollering at the ref, claiming that it was an intentional foul and that we should get the ball back after the free throw, but the ref didn't bite. Personally, I thought the ref had made the right call—I mean, it would have been nice to hold on to the ball, but from where I was on the court, it looked like a clean, hard foul.

The crowd was going wild but not too, too wild, because there were soldiers stationed throughout the arena, AK-47s on their shoulders, which kind of kept the crowd from getting out of control. This was the new Egypt, after all, but the military presence wasn't enough to kill the mood in the arena. The fans were into it and pulling for us, even if they were a little on the subdued side as Mohamed stepped to the line to take his shot. He bounced the ball a couple of times, took a couple of deep breaths, and the whole time I was thinking, *Please, Lord, please. Let this man make this one free throw.*

It wasn't a prayer so much as a plea.

My teammates were pleading, too—some of them were even down on their knees. That's how much these guys wanted to win this game.

Mohamed Ganesh was cool as cool could be. He sized up his shot and nailed it—swish.

My teammates on the bench went berserk, but the guys on the floor held back. Inside, in our heads, we were jumping up and down, but there were still three seconds on the clock. We still had some work to do.

Once again, Al-Ittihad looked to inbound the ball from beneath its own basket. This time they got the ball to their point guard, who should have probably sent the ball down the floor to another big man for a possible buzzer-beater, but that's not what happened. Instead, the point guard fired up a bomb from about halfway to half-court—a genuine Hail Mary. And, I swear it, the whole arena seemed to still and quiet as we watched this ball take a bulls-eye arc towards our basket. I don't mean to make it sound like a stupid, Disney movie cliché, to suggest that it felt like these last seconds were ticking off in slow motion, but we had a lot of time to watch that sucker fly across the court. A lot of time to think about what would happen if the shot fell.

But it didn't. It did hit the backboard, though, so our hearts sank for just a beat, but then the ball dropped to the floor, and they soared.

As one.

I fell to my knees and started crying. I don't know why exactly, but the tears just came pouring out. Nothing like that had ever happened to me on a basketball court before. I'd never shown that kind of emotion, and I'd played in some big games. But this wasn't just about the game, I realize now. It wasn't just about winning the championship. It was about accomplishing what I'd set out to do, to set things right, like I'd crossed a hundred miles of desert with a bucket of chicken and a milkshake and could finally, mercifully, breathe again. I could finally get back to the rest of my life.

My teammates were overjoyed, beside themselves. A couple of them ran over to me and picked me up off the ground, threw me onto their shoulders. A couple more ran over to Mohamed Ganesh and threw *him* onto their shoulders. Already the guys on the team loved this kid. He was always dancing on the team bus, making jokes, making trouble. He thought he was Kobe Bryant—he was his idol—and here he'd just carried us over a big damn hurdle, just like Kobe would have done.

As soon as we were back on the ground, I raced over to

Mohamed Ganesh and picked him up myself. Kissed him on the cheek—twice, the way I'd learned from my Egyptian friends. I said, "Thank you, man. Thank you."

He spoke a little bit of English. He said, "No, we do it for you. We do it for your family."

It was a beautiful, beautiful moment. It didn't change anything that was going on with my dad. It didn't erase any of the shit I'd had gone through to get to that point. It didn't set things right, all on its own.

But it was pretty damn sweet.

TEN | HOME

LONG STORY SHORT: I was named MVP of the postseason, which was a big, big deal. I got to kiss a championship trophy—also a big deal. Someone wrote an article about me for ESPN.com. There was a rally in Alexandria to celebrate our victory—the first basketball title in the history of the El-Olympi sporting club. Any other time, there might have been a parade, like they do it in the States, only there was enough unrest and unease going on with all those protests that the military didn't need to deal with a couple thousand crazed fans in the streets.

The biggest deal of all came when I called home the next morning and found out my dad had made some good progress overnight. My mother said things were looking better.

Just like that, we'd gone from bleak to hopeful.

I said, "What does that mean?"

She said, "He's awake. He's moving."

I told her I'd be home in the next day or so, but she said I should probably go to Atlanta first, to see Alexis. She didn't want me to see my father like that, I guess. Or maybe he didn't want me to see him like that. My brothers, they were still down in Atlanta, some of them, so we could all head up to Boston together, when the time was right.

Alexis met me at the airport in Atlanta. She hugged me so tight, I thought I would split open. She cried and cried. We both did—only she took the prize. Her tears just kept coming. She wasn't mad at me. That had only lasted a while. After a couple of days, she said, she'd understood, and by now she was past it. Now she was only happy.

I wanted to tell her everything all at once, but there was too much to tell. I couldn't think where to start, so we went for a walk instead. For a long time, we didn't talk at all. There would be time for all of that, I thought. Right now it was enough that we were together, at last.

A couple of days later, we went up to Boston to see my dad. He was home from the hospital, feeling pretty good. I don't think I was prepared to see him looking so frail, so old—but I guessed that was probably how I'd looked when I stumbled into Alexandria. He'd been through a lot, that's all. I reminded myself there'd been a time not too long ago when my father was ripped. He'd had muscles on top of muscles, strength on top of strength. One of his brothers had been a professional bodybuilder, and there were athletes up and down the many branches of our great family tree.

But here he was, almost like a shadow of the man I used to know. The only strength I could see now was a will to keep living. It was in his eyes, but you had to look for it, hard. It broke my heart to see him like this, but at the same time, my heart filled with gratitude just to be seeing him at all. Just to be back with my girlfriend, with my family. Just to be home.

I crossed the room to where my father was propped up in bed, against a bunch of pillows. I kissed him on the forehead.

I said, "I'm happy you're okay, Dad."

He looked me up and down. He'd known where I was, of course, what I'd been through—not all of it, but enough to think he might have lost me.

He said, "So, you decided to stay and play basketball." Not really asking, just saying.

I said, "Yeah, it ended up pretty good."

He said, "It always does."

ACKNOWLEDGMENTS

I WOULD LIKE TO THANK many people who helped me through the process of writing this book. To all who provided support, read, wrote, offered many comments and insights, and assisted in the editing and overall design of the book, I thank you from the bottom of my heart.

I would also like to thank my siblings—Joseph Jr., Anthony, Johnson, Justin, Malinda, and Melissa—for always believing in me and being positive role models in my life. You loved me and always made sure I was taken care of, no matter what, and for this, I love you guys. To Alexis Jones and the Jones family, thank you for all of your support during these difficult times in my life. God blessed me and put you in my life, and I am grateful for everything you have done. To my best friend, Ryan Ginnetty, thank you for believing in me and believing in this project. I thank you for being a great friend and for always being in my corner. To my friend Moustapha Niang, thank you for praying for me throughout my journey and for sticking with me through our most difficult times.

To my parents, Joseph Owumi Sr. and Claudia Owumi, thank you for always being tough on me and loving me at the same time. You let me go into the world and experience it for myself. Without the toughness you instilled in me, I wouldn't have been able to make it through, and for that I will love you both forever.

To God, you made everything possible. Thank you for always watching over me.

To Dan Paisner, thank you for helping me to write the book. You captured my voice and brought out my emotions within the story. You are a tremendous writer, and the sky is the limit for you. God bless you, and thank you, always.

I would also like to thank Alex Glass and John Silbersack and the entire Trident Media Group team for their hard work and support, and for setting everything in motion to get this book published. Thank you, too, to my editor Mark Weinstein and to his colleagues at Rodale, for their extra efforts in bringing this story out into the world. To Julian Rosenberg, Jared Schwartz, and the Caliber Media group, thanks for all your support during this project.

Finally, I would like to thank all of the people who have helped me throughout my journey during this chapter in my life. I will keep you in my prayers every day for the rest of my days. And to all the coaches, players, and friends who have helped me on my journey, thank you for taking the time out of your life to put the time into mine—God bless you all.

INDEX

An asterisk (*) indicates that a photo appears in the photo insert pages.

ABOUT THE AUTHORS

Alex Owumi was born in Lagos, Nigeria, and moved to the United States with his family at age eleven. He is one of seven children, and in 2008 he graduated from Alcorn State University. While at Alcorn State, he was twice named MVP of the basketball team and served as team captain his senior year. Unclaimed in the 2008 NBA draft, Owumi followed his dream of being a professional basketball player first in France, later in the US minor leagues, Macedonia, Libya, Egypt, and most recently in England. He currently lives in Atlanta but spent the 2012 season playing in England for the Worcester Wolves of the British Basketball League.

Daniel Paisner is the author of more than fifty books, on topics ranging from business and sports to politics and entertainment. He is also one of the busiest collaborators in publishing, having had a hand in the autobiographies and memoirs of some of our best-known athletes, actors, politicians, television personalities, and "ordinary" individuals who have managed to conquer extraordinary situations. He is coauthor of Serena Williams's *On the Line*; Denzel Washington's *A Hand to Guide Me*; Whoopi Goldberg's *Book*; Montel Williams's *Mountain, Get out of My Way*; and Geraldo Rivera's *Exposing Myself*—all *New York Times* bestsellers. He is also the author of the *New York Times* bestselling account of a New York City firefighter's epic tour of duty at the World Trade Center on September 11, 2001, *Last Man Down*, written with FDNY Battalion Commander Richard Picciotto, and the acclaimed Holocaust memoir *The Girl in the Green Sweater*, written with Krystyna Chiger. Paisner lives in Port Washington, New York, with his wife and three children.